WOMAN | OFFSIDE

WOMAN | OFFSIDE
A year with Lise Klaveness as she tries to reform football

MARIUS LIEN

FAIRPLAY
PUBLISHING

First published in 2024 by Fair Play Publishing
PO Box 4101, Balgowlah Heights, NSW 2093, Australia

www.fairplaypublishing.com.au

ISBN: 978-1-925914-10-8
ISBN: 978-1-925914-11-5 (ePub)

© Marius Lien 2024

The moral rights of the author have been asserted.
All rights reserved. Except as permitted under the *Australian Copyright Act 1968* (for example, a fair dealing for the purposes of study, research, criticism or review), no partof this book may be reproduced, stored in a retrieval system, communicated or transmitted in any form or by any means without prior written permission from the Publisher.

Cover design and typesetting by Leslie Priestley.
Front and back cover photographs of Lise Klaveness by Christian Belgaux.
The work of Lien and Belgaux was supported economically
by the freedom of speech organisation Fritt Ord.

This is an edited version of the original Norwegian text that was published in the magazine *Josimar 4/2023*. Quotes have largely been left to retain the English as a second language authenticity of the manuscript.
English translation by Marius Lien. Edited by John Coomer.

All inquiries should be made to the Publisher via hello@fairplaypublishing.com.au

NATIONAL
LIBRARY
OF AUSTRALIA

A catalogue record of this book is available from the National Library of Australia.

Contents

Prologue 1

1. Winter 3

2. Spring 18

3. Summer 54

4. Autumn 80

PROLOGUE

When Lise Klaveness entered Qatar's capital Doha in March 2022, only two things were missing: the donkey and the palm leaves. The newly elected Norwegian football president was about to give a speech during the FIFA Congress—and the expectations were enormous. A messiah for a corrupt football world, on her way into Jerusalem! For many football lovers, Klaveness represented something pure and unadulterated, without really having done anything special for it. As expected, her speech caused a stir.

"Our members demand change; they question the ethics in sport and insist on transparency. They are getting organised to make their voices heard. We must listen! We cannot ignore this call for change (…) The migrant workers injured or families of those who died during the build-up to the World Cup, should be cared for. FIFA, all of us, must now take all necessary measures to really implement change."

Immediately afterwards, the Honduran football president went to the podium, and stated that the congress was the wrong forum for that kind of talk.

The head of the Qatar World Cup was furious and criticised "Madame President" for not asking for a meeting in advance. FIFA president Gianni Infantino reacted with total silence. At least outwardly. However, back home in Norway, her speech was met with resounding applause. Klaveness received an honorary award from the free speech organisation Fritt Ord. The biggest newspaper, *VG*, which in the years before had given Qatar neither substantial criticism nor women's football the deserved support, wrote in the opinions section, "Klaveness' brave speech: Medicine in every word."

"Extreme courage," said culture minister Anette Trettebergstuen from the Worker's Party, a party who hardly raised its voice during the huge debate over boycott of the Qatar World Cup the previous year. Another big newspaper, *Bergens Tidende*, wrote, "Norway has become a country that finally dares to speak out properly."

Suddenly we were a nation of proud FIFA critics. The speech was quoted in media around the world and received strong praise in parts of the football community, for example, in England and Germany.

Klaveness continued speaking out during the World Cup itself. After Infantino's infamous *"Today I feel Arab"* speech - where he claimed that criticism of the Qatar World Cup was based on racism and colonial arrogance - she said that the FIFA president uses "the same rhetoric as dangerous and scary state leaders", according to Norwegian channel TV 2. She criticised him for failing to meet with her since he is, after all, "everyone's trustee". She also actively looked for an opponent to Infantino during the next FIFA presidential election but found none. Her year ended with a sprinkling of awards. Klaveness was, among a bunch of other things, chosen as Name of the Year in the newspaper *VG* and 'Bergen Citizen of the Year' in *Bergensavisen*—the newspaper from her hometown and Norway's second largest city, Bergen.

In Norway, and to a smaller degree internationally, this has created a view that Klaveness is a revolutionary who can fix everything that's wrong with football. The belief is a bit like Argentina simply playing the ball to Lionel Messi and then just sitting back, knowing that it will work out anyway. Argentina won the World Cup in Qatar using this method, but how much is really possible to accomplish in the football world as the football president in Norway?

For many years, I've worked as a journalist in the Norwegian football magazine *Josimar*. We've covered all parts of the game, including a long list of articles and one special issue about the Qatar World Cup. We've also looked extensively into the troublesome politics of world football, and the sport's dubious connection to all too many non-democratically elected state leaders.

For this book, I followed Klaveness for one calendar year (2023). At the start of the year, I asked what plans and ambitions she had for the next 12 months. I was by Klaveness's side throughout 2023 to document how her work to change the football world looks from the inside.

1
WINTER

At the end of January, a letter finds its way to Klaveness's mailbox at Ullevaal Stadium, the Norwegian national arena. She immediately publishes a post on Instagram about the letter, which is from Sanna and Victoria, two girls who have been walking around door to door in their neighbourhood to raise money for the fight for equality in football. They have managed to collect a small plastic bag of coins, which they sent with the letter to Ullevaal. In the Insta-video Klaveness says, "You have collected money so that we can continue to work on this topic, and we will do that." At the same time, the president is contacted by Norway's biggest stars: Ada Hegerberg, Maren Mjelde and Caroline Graham Hansen. They all produce small videos, saying they are excited about the girls' letter.

The incident sums up Klaveness's modus operandi. She constantly tries to create a kind of joint conversation between top football and the grassroot amateur footballers, to create the impression that everyone (including the biggest stars) plays on the same team and pulls in the same direction. She documents experiences, thoughts and ambitions through social media. She tries to keep the dialogue open in all directions—and she is concerned with gender equality. The latter in particular was likely to be a hot topic in 2023. But in January, when asked about objectives for the year, she refers to what the members of the Norwegian Football Federation (NFF) have decided that the board should work towards.

"We are elected representatives, acting according to a strategic plan," says Klaveness, and she sounds more like a dry bureaucrat than a saviour. She mentions four major issues that the board must "lean fully into, operatively, powerfully": barriers, facilities, equal opportunities and trust.

"Norwegian football has grown for 100 years, but now the numbers of players are going down. We have to do everything we can to turn this around, so that's first on the list. What are the barriers to participation? Why are the numbers dropping? There is no quick fix for this," she asserts, calling for information to understand why the numbers are dropping.

"I have never heard of any club that refuses people to come to training even if they can't afford to pay the club membership. We have arrangements for relenting. But people are proud, and I understand that, they don't want an unpaid invoice and they don't want to go and ask for help. Then we have the geopolitics in Europe, where the differences between people are increasing. Will this get better in 2025, 2030? No, it will obviously get worse. Then it becomes even more important that football is accessible to everyone. We have to spend time, effort and investment on this."

"Without increasing the number of employees at Ullevaal? Because that number has gone up, at least?" I ask.

"Yes, but we feel that we are understaffed. We do more and more and more."

"I find that I have to scroll further and further down the list of employees before I get to the press department, and this department grows every year."

"Yes, yes. I would like to create a project with some large partners where we could obtain five or 10 fully funded positions in some strategically selected grassroot clubs, who only work to understand what barriers there are in this particular club," she says, and moves to another major issue: pitches.

"The EU is about to introduce a ban on granular rubber in the month of February. At this time of the year, the natural grass pitches in Norway are closed because of snow and cold weather. But all over the country children and professionals still play football on artificial grass made of granular rubber."

"There are good reasons for the ban; it's terrible for the environment."

"Everyone wants environmentally friendly pitches, but we have no alternatives. Anyway, our standpoint is clear: [the] NFF wants to phase out granules as material for artificial pitches, that's not up for discussion. But it must happen in a way that doesn't limit the football activities and thus also limit something that's just as important when it comes to sustainability. We know that the football movement in Norway is dependent on artificial grass, professionals and grassroots. Many countries will suffer from a ban, but Norway will suffer the most. For 2023, an important goal is to work for good transitional arrangements. Stopping the largest popular movement in Norway is not sustainable. And the pitches don't become environmentally friendly when you start importing something, some birch or cork stuff that might not even work. Now, the business world will react. Whoever finds the replacement here will have a great business idea," she says.

Barriers, pitches—and thirdly on Klaveness's list of important topics for 2023 was equal opportunities.

"We have very few female coaches and football professionals [meaning not players, but specialists working in different areas within football]. We need girls and women to come out on the field as head coaches in the clubs around Norway. For the men, it must be natural to step aside and let the mothers take the session," says Klaveness, with reference to the children in Norway who are traditionally coached by voluntary parent coaches until their teens—and traditionally, that parent has been a man.

She also describes a challenge, namely that such discussions "become a bit like March 8 conversations" [International Women's Day]. "At the same time, there is a lack of secure knowledge about what one could do to actually improve the situation. So, we need to discuss it anyway."

But what about the sporting goals for 2023? Yes, they exist, like doing well in the Women's World Cup in Australia/New Zealand—"the most important event of the year" according to the president—and qualifying for the European Men's European Championship in 2024. Norway's participation in the U-21 European Championship in June/July of 2023 is already granted, so just being there will be one huge goal achieved. In the coming year, Klaveness will travel around the mountains and fjords of Norway, as well as to most of the continents on the globe. When this conversation takes place, she has just been to Kristiansund on Norway's windy west coast to visit the 'street team' made up of former drug addicts, alcoholics or other people who have had serious challenges in life.

"You should have been there! It was fantastic," says the president about the project that's been growing in Norway in recent years. Now all the top clubs in the country also run a street team.

One more thing about results: what about Norwegian clubs in the tournaments in Europe, does the president have any goals?

"On the women's side, it is only in the Champions League [CL] that there is economy."

"What do you mean?"

"We see how the women's football is getting professionalised. If you go far in the CL, you are left with quite a lot of money that your own and surrounding clubs will benefit from. Bodø/Glimt's success benefits all of Norway," she says about the club that has done well in the Conference and Europa Leagues in recent years, with their 6-1 victory against Rome one of the highlights.

"For women, only clubs that go to CL in Norway can make a profit, unless they have received subsidies from the NFF."

"But CL is not the only possibility. If the sponsors had stepped up on the women's side, that could also help?"

"I agree 100 percent. The most important thing is the situation locally. If Brann's women's team goes far in the CL, then the audience can really wake up, and then the sponsors will come ... The answer will always be found locally if we manage to create this eternal club affiliation with the women's side as well," she says.

Brann is the powerhouse club from Klaveness's hometown of Bergen. The club has some of the most dedicated supporters in the country, but until 2021 they didn't have a women's team. That year, the club that used to be the city's number one women's club—Sandviken, that Klaveness played for herself—became Brann. They won the league the first year and will play the Champions League in 2023-2024.

A Tool

So far, she has said nothing about FIFA or its president Gianni Infantino. Nothing about Qatar, corruption, electoral fraud, UEFA, migrant workers, compensation funds, money in brown envelopes and million-dollar transfers to Swiss banks. In other words, nothing about the issues that have given Klaveness the position she has in the field. The saviour sounds more like an average football worker.

"You haven't said anything about what you want to do at the FIFA Congress in Rwanda in March, or about the UEFA board where you will stand for

election during the UEFA Congress in April. Does that mean that the UEFA board and whatever you do in FIFA are just tools to achieve these goals?"

"Just right. The election is obviously important, but all the issues we work for internationally are these. And then we are keen to look into governance matters in a critical way because there are several things we find difficult to deal with internationally. It is difficult to understand the decision-making processes, and it is not open enough."

"What is a 'governance matter'?"

"For example, it seems as if the FIFA president can work directly towards individual states, without limits, as we have seen with Saudi Arabia," she answers.

Over the past few years, Infantino has spent a great deal of time in Saudi Arabia, a country that wants to position itself as a global football superpower through the organisation of championships, its presence as a sponsor and owner in clubs around the world, and by attracting famous stars to its own league. The state's purchase of Newcastle was widely debated around the world, and this transaction resulted in the Saudi flag being waved in the streets and stadium in the working-class city of Northern England. At the time of this conversation, Saudi Arabia has just been awarded the 2023 FIFA Club World Cup, and everyone expects them to apply to host the 2034 World Cup. It is also clear that Cristiano Ronaldo will end his career at Al Nassr in Riyadh—at this very moment, when we talk in late January 2023—like a solitary superstar, taunted by supporters because he's sacrificing everything for more cash.

"Saudi Arabia has a lot of money. And it's perfectly fair to have a lot of money. But we must have an organisation model where a chairman, like me or like Gianni, must have an arm's length distance from the players," Klaveness says, and has thus moved into the fourth 2023 ambition she mentioned at the beginning: trust.

"There is not enough transparency around governance and travel activity. The confederation presidents are busy with all sorts of other things, and then the FIFA presidential power becomes far too great. There is no real separation of powers, no arm's-length rules with which the rest of us can control the president. We are all at his mercy, and because of this the entire sports democracy can be undermined."

"An important principle in a democracy with distribution of power is that, through different institutions, everyone is held accountable. But how do you find someone the FIFA president is held accountable to?"

"No, in a way he's held accountable by everyone, and in a way, this turns out to be no one. When Infantino was elected, he and FIFA introduced many good things. For example, an independent governance committee, headed by Miguel Maduro. When Maduro and the committee did what they were supposed to do, and came up with troublesome suggestions, there was a quick change of leadership and the impression that the independency is gone. And then there is the lack of transparency, and the size of the board: it can become so large that it is not capable of decision-making. Then there are the rules, unwritten and written, that apply to how you can use the administration for your own candidacy," she says.

Even though it's more than a month away, everyone knows that Infantino will be re-elected as president at the FIFA Congress in Rwanda on March 16, as he is the only candidate in the election. It is also expected that there will be a proposal from one of the national presidents that Infantino's first term as president should be cancelled. This will give him the opportunity to sit even longer at the top.

"Didn't he get it cancelled already?" Klaveness asks.

Infantino took over after Sepp Blatter was forced to resign in 2016, following the investigations after the FBI raided the FIFA Congress in Zürich, Switzerland (more about that later). Thus, Infantino's first period was not a complete one, and has led to him saying that he didn't start until 2019.

"In any case, all these things are not something I can change alone," says Klaveness, and she returns to discussing the UEFA election, which is also her tool for changing FIFA. The UEFA Congress in Lisbon is on April 5. There, Klaveness will stand as a candidate for the board. She could have chosen to be a candidate for the one seat that's reserved for a woman. But instead, she went for one of the 'normal' seven board seats. So far in history, only men have been up for election for those seats.

"How do you run an election campaign? Do you travel around and meet the other presidents, who could potentially vote for you? Are you calling everyone by telephone? Talking to them at FIFA events and nice dinners?"

"I just spoke to the president of Hungary and had a simultaneous meeting with the presidents of Albania and Kosovo. It is a form I find easier. I feel that when you're going to mingle, you can mingle, not talk elections. When I talk to them in the meetings, I talk about the things I care about in my electoral platform. Grassroot football for women in Kosovo and things like that. It's a country we have collaborated with for many years. Yes, these countries are far behind in women's football, but the presidents there started on the women's side themselves and have ownership of it. They've received a lot of help from us, and they said it seemed as if I was concerned with the same things as my predecessors in Norway. So, they wanted to support me, they say that without me even asking about it," says Klaveness, who immediately after this interview will call another president for a similar conversation.

In other words, the election campaign is up and running.

"I try to create constructive conversations, so that a small movement can be created, which moves people a little. It will not be profitable for my election campaign, because it is obviously not good to speak loudly. Nobody does that. When no one does, it's because it's not a good idea. If I had done everything to get in, I would have been lying low, saying nothing."

"How many such presidential conversations have you had?"

"Let's see ... one, two, three, it was Lichtenstein and Estonia ... six ... maybe 10?"

"And who will vote for you?"

"I really have no idea about that. I also don't know if they will do what they say," she says.

In the past, Norwegian football leaders have talked a lot and warmly about 'Nordic cooperation'. About a Scandinavian block, an alliance that really can get things done in international football politics, if the block can only stand together. But now both Klaveness and the Danish president Jesper Møller are up for election. And there are many indications that Møller is not very enthusiastic about Klaveness's candidacy.

"The Nordic cooperation is still very good. This relationship is very much bigger than one individual against another individual. But there will be a little tension between us because I've realised that politics in UEFA is very regional. I haven't talked to anyone about it, but ..."

"Isn't it strange not to talk to the Danish president about this?"

"Yes, yes. I have tried, and it has to happen. The answer is that, quite literally, I have called him, yes, but he does not pick up the phone. Every time the media asks, he says that we have called each other in the past. But I have five or six unanswered messages from me to him. I am ghosted at the age of 41."

"Never too late!"

"Yes, it is a rejection. For me, it is quite an important principle that you must at least talk together," says Klaveness.

The Big Proposal

The first months of 2023 for Klaveness and the Norwegian Football Federation are characterised by the whole 'football family'—as football leaders like to call it, even though no one understands exactly who's part of this family and who's not—coming together on three occasions: first, the so-called "football assembly" in Norway, where representatives for the clubs in the federation gather at Ullevaal Stadium; then, the FIFA Congress in Kigali in Rwanda in March; and finally, the UEFA Congress in Lisbon in early April. Rwanda is the first congress after the World Cup in Qatar, which was massively criticised due to the host country's human rights violations and discriminatory treatment of workers. Norway has submitted a proposal for the FIFA Congress, dealing with Qatar and human rights.

"It's difficult to get the proposal through, but we believe it's important to file the proposal before the deadline, otherwise we won't be able to put it on the agenda," says Klaveness when I meet her in Oslo two days before the football assembly.

She also mentions that discreet conversations between various associations give the impression that many people liked this slightly rebellious move.

"We invite people to give input on the choice of words and try to create commitment. Then we can either withdraw the proposal, or adjust it, or we can get more supporters, which is of course our goal."

"The formulations in the proposal are largely about Qatar?"

"Yes, but also about the implementation of the human rights policy in general. We ask for two things. [First] that work is set up to assess whether

Article 6 of FIFA's human rights policy has been followed during FIFA's work with the Qatar World Cup. If not, how do we handle it? It is about remedy and working conditions in connection with the Qatar World Cup. And secondly, how should Article 6 be implemented in the time to come? After all, it is Qatar that is responsible for what happens there. You don't want to take that responsibility, but it follows from Article 6 that you have it," she says.

'You' in this case is 'FIFA'. Article 6 states that if FIFA in one way or another has contributed to the violation of human rights, then FIFA is obliged to compensate for that.

"How do we implement Article 6 in the future, for other tournaments and decisions?"

"Because Qatar does not exist in a vacuum?"

"Our attempt has been to be constructive. We have to talk about it, we have to have an analysis of it, and we have to try to clear our name," she says.

Clearing FIFA's name is one of the most difficult things you can try to do in the world today. The question is how all this will be received by FIFA's management.

"We spent a long time on the wording. How can we make it as clear as we can, but at the same time as vanilla as possible, so that it feels non-confrontational and doesn't become counterproductive," she says.

"And I feel we meet many countries that are positive [about it]."

"So, who has joined [with Norway]*?"*

"No, until now it's just us," she says, three weeks before Kigali.

"Didn't you say that people you meet are positive?"

"We are the ones raising and presenting it, but the UEFA group is continually asking for a meeting," she says, and goes into a small monologue about the complex political situation in football.

There is a UEFA group on human rights, which also works on responsibility after Qatar. The Norwegian Football Federation is part of this group, and this group would like to have meetings with FIFA about this issue. At the same time, Norway has come up with its own proposal.

"We have a kind of double track now," she says.

"And the person who manages that UEFA group hints that he doesn't like that we have a double track, and I was a bit upset that he didn't like it," says Klaveness.

Switzerland and Germany are the clearest supporters of Norway's proposal.

"The only thing we can be satisfied with will be that FIFA confirms that they are committed to doing this work, and that this work will be transparent. [If so], that's good, then none of us will make any noise in that congress. But there [still] is a long way to go, then," she says.

"Do you notice that people are working against you on this?"

"I wouldn't put it that way. Switzerland and Germany have a public that also are very concerned about these issues. But then, there may be other situations where I notice that I am, not exactly opposed, but ..."

"What about FIFA itself?"

"Yes, absolutely. After the speech last year, it has become like this: 'what do you intend to do this time?' But I don't understand how you expect to get changes implemented if you can't have friction in meetings. That it is seen as a declaration of war every time someone says something," she says.

"You can sit and talk, but as soon as there is a certain formality about it, there is a very strong culture of fear. People are afraid of losing control, afraid of their positions, afraid of losing the possibility to host tournaments or international games," she says before she must finish the interview because she has a scheduled telephone meeting with a European football president.

Later in the evening, she calls me to finish our talk, as we agreed, and she is full of energy.

"It is simply the best conversation I have ever had with any other president. We talked for a long time about Gianni Infantino's re-election. He was shaken by the appointment of Noël La Graët as CEO of the Paris office of FIFA," she says.

La Graët was football president in France for many years but had to step down at the end of February due to serious accusations of sexual harassment. On the same day he met the press about his departure, La Graët said that Infantino had promised him a job as head of FIFA's office in Paris.

"We talked more about the integration of Muslim girls into football. We haven't figured out how to do that properly in Norway yet, but there are some clubs in his home country that get it right. Then the question was our concerns for the future. Even though Infantino will be re-elected, it is important to work with the small things, and influence the direction. Then we'll see if his board agrees to support our proposal. But if he agrees to go out and challenge Infantino ...," she says, leaving the sentence hanging in the air.

A Toast for the President

It is March, and it's time for the so-called football assembly in Norway: the day when representatives of all the football clubs in the country can go to Ullevaal Stadium and meet both the national leaders and each other. They can wine, dine and participate in the sports democracy through voting on different issues on the agenda.

In 2021, the assembly was dominated by the Qatar World Cup, and the big question was if Norway should boycott the tournament. The issue was so big and complicated that the delegates decided that another extraordinary football assembly was needed in the summer of 2021, where only one question was up for debate: if Norway should boycott or not.

Before that, a special committee nominated by the NFF was to present a report about the Qatar World Cup. The result was weeks of fierce, polarised debate. The NFF was accused of trying to manipulate clubs into voting to go to Qatar, while the FIFA-critical organisations became club members, so that they could persuade clubs to vote against going to Qatar. The neutrality of the NFF report was heavily questioned.

At that time, Klaveness was head of the top football section in the NFF, not football president. In the beginning, she supported a boycott. However, when it was time for voting, she had made a U-turn, and recommended the clubs vote against a boycott. And that became the final result. But the assembly also instructed Norway's football president to speak up about the human rights situation for the World Cup workers in Qatar, and also to demand a more transparent and less corrupt FIFA. Additionally, the assembly produced a list of 26 NFF human rights demands for World Cup workers in Qatar for FIFA and the Supreme Committee to fulfil. These 26 points received a solid dose of ridicule—many supporters voiced that in their opinion, neither FIFA nor the Supreme Committee were going to give a shit about 26 demands from Norway about human rights.

Nevertheless, before the next football assembly, Klaveness had become the new president. The first thing she did was to give her famous speech in Doha during the FIFA Congress in 2022.

In the last couple of weeks, Klaveness has visited the county federation of Finnmark which is the northernmost region in Norway; she has spent a day with another street team; she has been to France to see Norway's women's national team; she posted an Insta-story in support of Ukraine against Russia and Vladimir Putin—even though she, and everyone else involved in football, is playing on the same team as Putin, at least if we're to believe what was said in the broadcast conversation between Gianni Infantino and Putin during the World Cup in Russia in 2018. She has also given a long interview to British newspaper *The Observer*, among other things.

Eivind Kopland from the NFF's ethics committee takes the podium and describes a "paradigm shift" that he believes has taken place after Klaveness became president. He talks about the "courageous and brutally honest" speech in Doha. He raises the point that Klaveness mentioned on the very popular Friday night talk show *Lindmo* the night before—that the orange soccer ball she refers to in the Doha speech smelled so bad that even her cat jumped out of bed. Kopland says, "a lot of deserved praise has been directed at Lise Klaveness in the last year," before he states that the NFF's ethics committee puts a "solid seal of approval" behind the work the NFF has done in the last year.

The discussion goes on and on. One peculiarity with the Norwegian football organisation is that the NFF organises both the professional leagues and players, as well as eight to nine divisions of amateur football and tens of thousands of child players around the country—grassroot football as it is called in Norway. Thus, the president has to deal with the needs of both international superstars such as Erling Braut Haaland and Ada Hegerberg, as well as the needs of six-year-old girls and boys across the country. As a result, the assembly debate deals with things such as grassroots versus professionals, rubber granules, the dwindling numbers of football players in Norway, amateur contracts, climate neutrality and sustainability, and not least: how early should the bigger, stronger clubs actually start hunting for players in the smaller neighbouring clubs around Norwegian cities?

"Are we on our way into the wombs to find the greatest talents early enough?" asks delegate Torkjell Johnsen from the northern club Porsanger IL from the podium.

"People watch TV instead of playing football," says Lise Klaveness during her speech, referring to the problem of declining player numbers in Norwegian football. As Lise and the others discuss this problem on the podium, the delegates in the hall stream Arsenal-Bournemouth or Chelsea-Leeds matches from the Premier League on their iPad screens.

Klaveness updates her own Instagram account with various stories throughout the evening. Nothing happens on the NFF's official account. A sigh of disappointment goes through the hall right before the evening fun starts, when the speaker states that the assembly will start up again at 09:00 the next day, and not at 09:30 as announced.

Between all the delegates who approach the president to rub shoulders with her, Klaveness tells *Josimar* about an email from a European president who not long ago promised her support in the UEFA elections. Now the president says that this position must not be made public. And the election itself in UEFA is secret. So far, no one has come out publicly in support of her. In other words, it is impossible to know how the elections will go.

Over the course of the evening at Ullevaal, it is obvious that absolutely everyone in the hall strongly supports Klaveness. She is tough. Brave. As strange as it might seem, this is the same hall and crowd that voted against Norway boycotting the World Cup in Qatar one-and-a-half years earlier. The same crowd that did not create any significant disagreement when Klaveness's predecessor Terje Svendsen ran the NFF for years together with the then secretary general Pål Bjerketvedt, and before them the leading duo was Kjetil Siem and Yngve Hallén—none of them ever said one critical word against FIFA. But now everyone is standing behind Klaveness. The entire Norwegian 'football family' has moved to the right side of history.

The NFF's secretary general in 2023 is Karl-Petter Løken—a civil engineer and former winger for the national team and Rosenborg BK in the beginning of the club's golden period that included a run of 13 league titles in a row, as well as significant success in the European Cups. According to the word on the street, he too has contributed to this strange new atmosphere in the NFF. For example, both he and Lise speak to volunteers in Norway's clubs as equals. They don't 'talk down' to them like their predecessors did.

Comedian Christian Mikkelsen is master of ceremonies during the dinner, and a discussion at our table arises: who provided the entertainment last year? Was it another comedian? Or was it a singer? Names are thrown over the table, including some of Norway's biggest artists, but no one remembers. After a three-course meal, Klaveness gives the traditional after-dinner speech.

She starts by saying that she is a vegetarian, and also terrible at cooking. She mentions that she's been invited to appear on a popular reality show called *Champion of Champions* several times, where former sports champions meet to compete and play, but she's always turned down the offer. But when she was asked by another show, *Four-Star Dinner*, she said yes. This was a concept—celebrities cooking dinner—that was so far from who she really was that she agreed. Inevitably, it ended in an embarrassment, but she has nevertheless chosen to summarise the previous year, 2022, through a 'food narrative and filter' in her speech. So here we go—what can represent her speech in Doha? "Fried tarantulas," says the football president, and the crowd burst out laughing; she has them all on board. She invites a bunch of close colleagues to give their own illustrations of 2022 through the same food narrative and filter. Mikkel Mørk Solli from the Vålerenga club chose the VAR, which he compares to "Japanese fusion". Lise agrees. "It looks good, but it tastes like crap". More examples follow.

Afterwards, we're into extra time—more drinks and a DJ takes over from the speeches—and it's only fun, no work, until the wee hours.

The next day at 10:00, Klaveness takes the podium again to introduce a proposal to change the NFF's international strategy. As mentioned earlier, during the extraordinary assembly to discuss the potential Qatar boycott, a list of 26 points were agreed upon for the NFF to send to FIFA. These points were also to be the guidelines for the NFF's international steps in the coming years. For example, the president was instructed to take the podium at every FIFA Congress, a tradition that Klaveness began with her famous Doha speech. However, after a year in international football, she believes that taking the podium every year would be counterproductive. Through the new strategy she presents, which also contains a separate human rights policy, she wants more freedom to decide her own actions.

Right after she asks the assembly's permission to not give a speech every year, the delegate from Trane strides to the podium and says that the new proposal from the president is perfectly fine for him. Her proposal is adopted unanimously.

"It was good that the guy from Trane FK came up," says Klaveness.

"He has been one of the important voices in the Qatar debate."

"After all, last year it was his suggestion that we should go to the podium every year. But that would be a bit like wearing handcuffs. This year, for example, it will not be a smart move to go to the podium at the FIFA Congress. It won't help the matters we care about. We will have to consider that every year. And he said, live from the podium, 'yes, you will have to consider that.'"

2
SPRING

"It was great," says Lise, referring to the Royal Palace the day before—March 8, International Women's Day.

"Lots of women there, from 34 to 94 years old. They have good speech writers at the Palace. They say everything that is politically correct, but it is better than nothing. The content is good and relevant," says Klaveness, before mentioning some of the prominent guests: journalist Hege Duckert spoke to everyone, Ann-Kristin Olsen (the first female governor of the Svalbard islands, close to 1,000 kilometres north from the Norwegian mainland) was there. Olsen has a book called *My Life as a Man*. "A very good book," Lise says, about the book whose title plays with all the professional titles Olsen had through her working career, all of them ending with '…man'.

The grand old jazz singer Karin Krogh performed, and next to Klaveness at the table was the queen on one side and 'the mother of the motherland', Gro Harlem Brundtland, on the other. Brundtland was Norway's first female prime minister, a position she held for three separate periods. No government has ever had as many women in it as Brundtland's and she is considered one of the most prominent politicians in modern Norwegian history.

"There, as well, in that company, the speech is an icebreaker," says Klaveness.

The speech she's referring to of course is the one she gave in Doha in front of FIFA and the rest of the world.

"Several of these pioneer women are interested in the speech, especially immigrants. This is very good to hear. My strong experience is that those who are absolutely most excited about Norwegian leaders speaking up against discrimination that happened during the Qatar World Cup, and feel most emotionally connected to it, are immigrant women. People from Nepal and surrounding countries. Gianni made an attempt to play the East against the West," she says, with reference to Infantino's infamous "Today I feel Arab" speech on the opening day of the World Cup.

Let's take a quick look back at Infantino's time in the FIFA president's chair. As already mentioned, the FIFA Congress in Zürich was raided by the FBI in 2015. Following the subsequent trials, several football executives were arrested, suspended and banned from football. FIFA president Sepp Blatter had to step down. The FBI's findings showed that corruption was an important reason why Qatar won the World Cup. Before the FIFA elections in 2016, Infantino was the secretary general of UEFA, but at the same time an unknown name to many. His election campaign was active and ubiquitous, and he was particularly good at making agreements with African and Caribbean confederations. If you have the whole of Africa behind you in such an election, you are already close to victory, since it is a continent with so many member states. Infantino won—and he quickly began to secure his position. He made sure to install obedient supporters in important positions, including a new president of the Confederation of African Football (by FIFA illegally interfering in CAF's elections) and a new secretary general of FIFA: Fatma Samoura.

Samoura was soon stripped of the responsibilities her predecessors had held, giving Infantino much greater power. He removed the two leaders of the ethics committee, i.e. FIFA's internal legal body, which is supposed to ensure that the football organisation follows its own rules and remains uncorrupted. He was being investigated by the leaders he removed for at least two matters: using the private plane of the Russian oligarch Alisher Usmanov for meetings under the auspices of FIFA, and for interfering in election campaigns for independent confederations such as CAF.

"Now, hundreds of cases are going to be put on hold," said the outgoing ethics chairman immediately after the replacement. Infantino soon became an avid supporter of the Qatar World Cup. A couple of years before the event, Infantino moved to Doha. He has travelled countless times to Saudi Arabia and arranged for this country to buy into world football. He posed on commercial videos promoting tourism in the country, dancing with traditionally dressed men with swords in hand—in a country that is known to execute people through beheading them with swords. According to sources inside FIFA, Infantino has spent more time in Riyadh than in his other home town (Zürich) in recent years. Communication with the press has been limited to short, sometimes bizarre press conferences, and otherwise he has spoken through decrees and press releases.

The "Today I feel Arab" speech Klaveness referred to was given on the World Cup's opening day, and the message was that criticism of the Qatar World Cup based on the human rights situation in the country and its treatment of migrant workers was racist and colonialist. Infantino presented himself as a spokesperson of the oppressed, representing the broad strata of the people of the Arab and African world.

However, Klaveness's experience, based on how immigrant women responded to her Doha speech, suggests the opposite.

Slovenia

It has been less than a day since the celebration at the Palace, and Klaveness has moved to Slovenia, the home country of UEFA president Aleksander Čeferin. She has already met with the country's football association, and I talk to her over the phone.

"The proposal we will present in Kigali was not a topic. But people always talk about the speech in Doha. There's always jokes about it. If there are friendly relations, watch out now! Lise is going to speak again!"

"The speech was mentioned quite a few times in the Norwegian football assembly as well?"

"It has become a platform. When I spoke for the Fare network, an organisation that works against discrimination, there were a lot of young leaders from various anti-discrimination organisations present. People are very concerned about that speech. They identify it with their struggles. For example, a person who worked on the hijab ban in France, on the inclusion of minority women in football. The speech lives its own life. It was very much aimed at an audience that was at a congress, but it has turned into something else, and become a bridge to different environments," she says.

It has also led to Norway having to sweep its own door. During an event a couple of weeks earlier, for example, she met with people from the organising committee of the Qatar World Cup and from various Muslim countries. Among other things, they brought up the Kongsberg Group weapons factory which sponsors Norwegian sports, as well as selling weapons to Israel and other countries at war. That's sportswashing the Norwegian way.

"I like it," says Klaveness, about being challenged in such a way.

"You just had a meeting in the UEFA group that works with human rights. Did you agree upon something?"

"It's about following up Qatar to see if they do as [they] promised, and it will be difficult. In a way it's helpful. Helpful and frustrating. Tomorrow Norway will meet the FIFA sub-committee for human rights, which we didn't know existed, an independent human rights committee in FIFA. One of the 26 points from the Norwegian football assembly was to work to get such a committee set up. We have asked about it many times but have never received an answer. But when we submitted the proposal to Kigali just now, we heard that the sub-committee for human rights, yes, it is up and running. President Michael Llamas of Gibraltar chairs the committee. We are keen to find out who they are, when it was created, what they do and how we work."

"What about the proposal, what will happen to it in Kigali?"

"We have gotten Germany with us. It's good, they are a heavy country. Otherwise, people are anxious to join something, even if everyone agrees on the content. It is surprising to see that the proposal is seen as such a strong utterance, that it gets counterproductive. We believe, however, that it is useful if more countries go together with more force. Since we agree upon the content."

"You say that everyone agrees upon the content?"

"It is a reasonable proposal. Not a verbal hand grenade. We propose that an assessment should be made of something that is highly debated. It is a tough matter. And it is not easy to know what kind of results one can achieve. We hope FIFA agrees to make an assessment, that they commit to something in that direction."

"Now I'm disappointed with other good countries, with Nordic neighbours, who I had wished were more clearly involved in getting this onto the agenda, including in formal arenas in FIFA. I don't understand why it is like that. But it's about fear of losing relationships and real assignments you apply for, and things like that," she says.

During the UEFA Congress in April, the European Women's

Championship 2025 will be awarded. The bid from the Nordic countries is one of the favourites to win. Switzerland is another.

"We are constantly told that it is better to work behind closed doors. We say yes, we will work behind closed doors. But would there have been any activity behind the closed doors if no one did some work outside as well, completely open? People say to us, as an argument against the proposal: it is much better to go together than alone. Then we say yes, that's why we're asking for support for something everyone in the group agrees on. Then we don't have to come and present something that is only from us alone. We talk in circles, it's incredibly frustrating," she says, around two weeks before the FIFA Congress in Kigali.

According to Klaveness, it is now the Kigali Congress that keeps the discussions about Qatar's legacy alive. If not for the congress and the opportunities that the proposal can create, the spark would have died long ago.

"Ever since the speech, there has been political strain, we have been a little isolated for a year. How can we show what we mean without isolating ourselves further? It ends up in completely banal stuff. Infantino is to be re-elected. I think it will happen by acclamation. We are not voting for him. But we have respect for the congress and democracy, and we cannot just be grumpy. Still, it's important that we don't clap, even though he's elected. It's a banal thing, but we must use those small opportunities we have to communicate what we think about FIFA's leadership and all those unfulfilled expectations," she says.

This is the climate of free speech in the 'football family' in 2023. The only thing you are allowed to do in protest is not clap. According to Klaveness, most people will do as expected, and welcome the president for another term.

"There are a handful of nations who, like us, will leave the clapping to the others."

Kigali, March 14, 15:15 pm

TV channel TV2 is in place in Rwanda's capital, Kigali, and Klaveness signs a new cooperation agreement with Vietnam. Klaveness's adviser Magnus

Borgen leads her, secretary general Karl-Petter Løken, an interpreter and TV2 out onto the veranda to get the best possible background for the shots. Then there are meetings. Meetings, meetings and more meetings. Romania doesn't have time; can Lise call him? Try to meet him?

Karl-Petter Løken interrupts. "The Romanians have problems with granules too, they are not allowed to water in the summer due to drought, so the grass won't grow."

"Can I make it happen? Between Marriott and the game?" Klaveness asks.

"Is it possible to nudge Kosovo a little?" Borgen asks.

"I have spoken to them, they are good," says Klaveness.

"The Balkan people are important!"

"And the Baltics."

"Montenegro! That's the old Milan player. Haven't you played with him, KP?"

"Latvia? We need to take on Luxembourg."

"Armenia, Azerbaijan, I have to ask there," says Lise.

And so the talk goes on as the clouds darken. Rwanda's rainy season has just begun. On the same day, Norwegian ace and Lyon striker Ada Hegerberg posts a video in collaboration with Amnesty, in which she reads a letter from a Nepali widow of a migrant worker who died before the World Cup. The video ends with a call for FIFA to pay compensation to those left behind so they are not trapped in debt to the agents and companies that hired them. In other words, about the same as the NFF and Klaveness are asking for in their proposal. But what will the proposal lead to? According to Lise, the "best-case scenario" is that FIFA comes with a formal obligation to follow up on Article 6 of the statutes, as well as follow up on the rights of workers through a compensation fund and other means. But will FIFA do this?

Towards the end of the day, Klaveness and co. believe that yes, at least they will commit to do the assessment Norway is asking for in the proposal, presumably through a statement recorded on video. The NFF has demanded that FIFA's statement contains some fixed, controllable points. If the statement isn't clear enough then ... everyone remembers the speech from last year.

Back home in Norway, Klaveness has repeatedly said that she will not take the podium this time, but not everyone believes her. In fact, it seems that the mere thought of another speech from the NFF president or other presidents is so terrifying that FIFA would rather make a statement containing the necessary points.

Kagame at the Back

It is the day before the day, and time for the regular football tournament where the various confederations play against each other: FIFA against UEFA against CAF against CONMEBOL and so on. Klaveness is number 2 on UEFA's team, and a couple of Rwandan teams are also competing. The press is invited, but no one is allowed to enter the stadium gates. Why? No one knows. The first matches are played in front of empty stands and have a huge security presence. Eventually the doors are opened, and the explanation for the exclusion is Paul Kagame. He is the president of Rwanda who has been in office since 2000 and never received less than 90 percent of the vote in elections. On this day, he played on CAF's team in the tournament, which lost 3–2 against FIFA, where Infantino played wearing number 9.

Kagame grew up in Uganda, but returned to Rwanda as an adult, pursuing a military career. Towards the end of the 1980s he joined the RPF, the Rwandan Patriotic Front, which at first was an organisation for Tutsi refugees and later became a military resistance group. In 1990, civil war broke out. The RPF, then under Kagame's leadership, fought the Hutu-dominated government. On April 7, 1994, president Habyarimana was killed when the plane he was in was shot down. The extreme Hutu group Interahawme took control of the country, and immediately launched a carefully planned genocide that lasted until July 15. During this period, between 800,000 and one million Tutsi and moderate Hutus were killed, most with machetes and clubs or shot. The genocide ended when the RPF and Kagame gained the upper hand in the civil war, seizing control of the country. Since then, Rwanda has gone through an arduous and apparently successful process of reconciliation. Now the country is a model to follow with insights that are exported to other nations where ethnic groups stand against each other. In 2023, the country appears harmonious. The antagonisms between Hutu and Tutsi—which were first created by the German and Belgian colonial powers—have disappeared.

But countries in Eastern Europe during the Cold War also appeared harmonious, as dictatorships often do. And presidents also need security. Not least those who always win elections with almost 100 percent of the votes. When Kagame has left the stadium, the doors open, and I find Klaveness.

"Did you win?"

"Of course we did," she says, as she stands on the sidelines among former world champions and now Infantino loyalists such as Cafu (Brazil) and Christian Karembeu (France). The sideline conversation is like those for most grassroot matches.

"Did you get anything done on the pitch?"

"You gained a few kilos too much since last year?"

According to the NFF's team, Klaveness completed at least one successful stepover feint. Senegalese Khalibou Fadiga approaches her.

"Lise! How did it go?"

"Well, what do you think?" she says.

"We've studied together," she explains, after a cheerful chat. A university in France and UEFA has arranged it so that a top playing career can have academic value as a bachelor's degree, after which one can go on to a master's in sports leadership. Klaveness and Fadiga have done this master's degree with people like Didier Drogba and Kaka in the same group.

"We have been to Old Trafford and other big arenas on study trips together, all over Europe. I think he [Fadiga] supports the Infantino line, but we are all human beings, disagreements aren't dangerous, and we [have] become friends," she says.

The rain has started to pour down, and lightning strikes the pitch. The rest of the matches are cancelled, and as we stroll across the artificial grass— the artificial turf is a FIFA requirement in green Kigali where it rains five to six months a year—Infantino gathers a couple of hundred Rwandan children behind him in a well-organised photo shoot. Look at me, friends with all the children of Africa!

An hour later, the closed UEFA meeting is finished. The presidents and general secretaries hurry to the FIFA dinner. But one person remains and talks, first to the right, then to the left. Lise Klaveness. Now she is talking about the Nordic application to organise the European Championship for women in 2025. An application which, like her candidacy for the UEFA board and the NFF proposal, also needs support.

When Klaveness and the presidents go to dinner, there's no room for journalists. Instead, the photographer and I choose to go to a networking session disguised as a cocktail party, organised by Rwanda's Ministry of Sports.

"Rwanda is taking over the world of sports," shouts one of the government's representatives from the stage.

"We are the biggest sports hub in Africa," shouts another.

Mingling and the exchange of information is encouraged, which happens with advisory corps constantly coming over and talking about developments: AfroBasket 2021 was held in Rwanda, Visit Rwanda (the country's tourism board) sponsors Arsenal and Paris Saint-Germain, and various other applications for championships are in.

"The fact that FIFA brought the congress here is a great victory," says one of the government's press people to our table.

Rwanda therefore uses sport in the same way as Qatar: to show off a successful, peaceful and well-functioning country as a temptation for tourists, that it's a chilled-out haven in a troublesome region. No one at the event wants or can talk about the absent freedom of the press and the many illegally imprisoned journalists, like Theonestse Nsengimana. Or about the torture and murder of Kagame's political opponents or about the terror sentence and the unfair trial against Paul Rusesabagina, the hero of the 1994 genocide—all of this is discussed by, among others, Human Rights Watch.

"Who Am I to Give Up?"

The congress hall is full of football jerseys. Custom-made shirts act as national nameplates, they hang above the chairs, three for each country. A little walk around the floor shows that Klaveness is by no means the only one who raised eyebrows when FIFA's sub-committee on human rights appeared out of nowhere. Several presidents from heavy central European federations say the same thing before the actual congress starts—suddenly the committee was there, and they know nothing about it yet.

"A little less nervous now than last year?"

"Well, but FIFA has said that they will commit, the exciting thing is how they do it," says Klaveness.

"We have this one here, just in case," general secretary Karl-Petter Løken says with a smile and showing a sheet of paper with the inscription 'Request to Speak'. It can be held up if you wish to speak during the congress.

Everything is prepared, the NFF will not applaud, neither will Germany and a couple of others.

Infantino goes to the podium: "Dear excellency, Mr. President, my dear brother Paul Kagame". He tells a story about when he was in Rwanda in 2016 to run for election as FIFA president after Sepp Blatter had just lost his job due to alleged corruption. Infantino announced his candidacy. A classic football election campaign followed, with the candidates flying from country to country to gather support. Kagame had welcomed Infantino to Rwanda but said, "Sorry—I'm not going to vote for you."

With a heavy heart, Infantino planned to go to a football match. The then UEFA secretary general was unable to get a ticket for the match, so Infantino's mood sank even further. He decided to give up his entire pursuit of the FIFA presidency. Then a stranger suddenly came over with a ticket to the Kigali Genocide Memorial—the mass grave, memorial and museum that tells the story of the 1994 genocide. Infantino thanked him for the ticket, dropped the football game and went to the museum—it describes all the atrocities in horrifying detail, including how children were tortured, thrown against the wall and hacked to death with machetes. "And after that I thought, who am I to give up?" He decided to continue his election campaign, and the rest is history.

Then Kagame is introduced in grandiose terms. Two days earlier, Infantino presented him with an award for the important role the Rwandan president plays in the development of African football. Kagame says in return, "thank you to FIFA for choosing to put the congress in Rwanda," and goes on to talk about the "hypocritical" criticism of the World Cup in Qatar. A type of criticism that was "racist", that had no other goal than to keep Africa and the rest of the world out of good company, but fortunately, under Infantino's exceptional leadership, he declared that the event was a success.

FIFA secretary general Fatma Samoura carries out one of her few permanent tasks—she calls out all the federations in the room: 208 out of 211 member states are present.

During the review of the finances, Infantino repeats countless times that FIFA's income has gone from 6.4 to 7.4 billion dollars in the last year. In the next four-year period, it will go up to 11.5, he promises. "And in that account, the Club World Cup is not included, so there will probably be a couple of billion more (...) Then I have to remind you that when I took over, the equity was one billion dollars. Today, it is 4 billion," he says. Both the agenda for the congress and the financial report are approved.

Infantino must be in doubt about what the audience thinks about Qatar, because he calls it "the best World Cup ever". But the day before, trade union BWI released a report stating that the reforms for the workers stopped right after the World Cup ended. However, during the congress, FIFA claims that these reforms are implemented in new places every day.

Then there's the election. The chairman of the meeting says that Infantino's first presidential term started in 2019. Infantino says the same. Although he said an hour-and-a-half earlier that he ran an election campaign in Rwanda in 2016. Nevertheless, now it seems to be formalised: Gianni Infantino's first term has been cancelled. He started in 2019. Three terms are the maximum length for a FIFA president, and this means that he can stand for re-election in 2027 and sit until 2031.

Infantino is the only candidate. He is applauded by the entire hall. Almost. Some refrain from clapping: Norway, Germany and a couple of others. More than three, less than ten.

"To all of you who love me, I know there are many. To all you haters, I know there are a few. I love you all. Especially today," is the newly elected president's comment. "We love you too, president," shouts Fatma Samoura. The audience applauds.

The last point on the agenda is Norway's proposal. Gibraltar's president Michael Llamas, the head of FIFA's sub-committee for human rights, says that they were just a working group at first, and then, around Christmas they were upgraded to be the long-requested sub-committee. After another round of bragging about Qatar, he gets to the point: there is a slight disagreement regarding Qatar. The perspective of the NFF is partially recognised. The committee promises to produce a report examining the points in Norway's proposal. They're going to follow up on Article 6 of FIFA's human rights policy, saying that FIFA shall not "cause or contribute to adverse human rights impacts". They are also going to create a fund for survivors of dead workers.

"It was the best we could hope for, to get a commitment from FIFA on the biggest stage," says Klaveness afterwards.

She is surrounded by the media: the Danish-Norwegian collaborators Idrettspolitikk/EkstraBladet ask the questions, while Norwegian media NRK, TV2, *VG* and Aftenposten hold the microphones. Later, internationals like the BBC, RFI and a few more follow. She is not even halfway through before the other delegates have left. I have a question, right at the end—"two minutes, maximum," says adviser Magnus Borgen, never more than ten centimetres away from the boss.

"You say you are satisfied with the response from Llamas and FIFA. But the stuff they communicated at the start of the congress was the complete opposite through the mutual embrace between Kagame and Infantino, and Kagame saying that the criticism of Qatar is hypocritical. How are we supposed to know what FIFA really means?"

"Good observations, and it's good that it becomes apparent. That is world football's great dilemma. People raise their political flags in different directions. I know that the African continent is very concerned with anti-racism, and a very large part of the criticism against Qatar is that it is a racist system ... but the challenge is that you give the stage to a head of state, unchallenged, who says something that at least I disagree with."

"And then there will be a kind of unity between what FIFA thinks and what he thinks?"

"It will appear as a unity. Identification. It's not good, it's nothing new. This is part of the reason why we do not support Infantino; all the way there is a tendency to play Europe against the rest, and a lack of arm's-length distance to state leaders. What Llamas does is try to get everyone together, he praises what has been, perhaps too much, but the important thing is what they commit to. That he recognises human rights as part of what football is and should do," says Klaveness, who had actually planned a visit to the Kilagi Genocide Memorial before the congress—i.e. the place that inspired Infantino in 2016. But it had to be cancelled.

"I have written my juridical master's thesis on the international genocide decision, as well as the court settlement about the genocide in Rwanda. I feel like I've been to Rwanda many times, even though I haven't. It was a little sad that I didn't get to go to that memorial. As for what Infantino said, I really like to interpret people in the best sense. At the same time, he has a way of speaking that is difficult to associate with."

The Press Conference

"Some of you are so mean. Why are you so mean? Why? I can't understand it," says Infantino, with hurtful eyes. In front of him sits 40–50 journalists. "Unfortunately, because of a few of you, all of you have to listen to another monologue from Gianni Infantino," he continues. "You should write more about football, and less about the football administration. I received more than 200 letters of approval before the election. I got a standing ovation here today." Nevertheless, says the president, the same old criticism comes from the media. He signals that in his eyes the journalistic criticism of FIFA is a personal attack on him, almost a vendetta, and again: the criticism against Qatar is racist. The monologue goes on and on.

After twenty minutes, it is time for questions. A forest of hands shoots up in the air. FIFA's press director selects the lucky ones, and the president must answer a couple of questions about football's development in Africa, one about Saudi Arabia's attempt to sponsor the Women's World Cup, and two more. Then it's over. The monologue took three quarters of the time, and 95 percent of the journalists were not allowed to ask their prepared questions.

Before Departure

Back at the hotel, the meetings are underway again. Lithuania, Kazakhstan, Portugal and Austria are on the agenda.

I go back to my own residence, take a nap, and return a couple of hours later. Klaveness sits in the sofa group at the reception and talks to NRK. Another federation is waiting, and another TV2 interview is on the way. The flight is approaching. Klaveness walks over to my table, and repeats that she is happy—happier than she had dared to be. With the sub-committee and the reaction to Norway's proposal, something tangible has been brought up that must be used in the future. It's a small step, but at least it is a step. She has booked 10 new meetings in the next few hours, before the flight home to Norway leaves late at night.

"What do you think of FIFA's boss saying journalists are "mean"?"

"That is part of the reason for our decision not to vote for him. Even if it didn't have any effect that we didn't applaud, it is important for us to give those kinds of signals we have available. He has used press conferences and other occasions to say that the critics are racists, which is wrong and a bit scary. It shows that FIFA is a closed organisation, and it is stressful. It creates an untidy, unclear culture where you ultimately don't know how decisions are made."

"Was there any discussion among your talking partners about his handling of the press?"

"Yes. As matter of fact, there was. It has been like this for a while, and it is confirmed that this is on the wrong track," she says.

"Is FIFA allowed, according to its own rules, to simply announce that the period he set from 2016 to 2019 does not count?"

"He is using the fact that the first period was not complete. It is a legal question which has not been tried before. Extending periods and making himself difficult to reach is classic for a president who retains power more and more unchallenged," she says.

A review of FIFA's regulations does not provide a clear answer. The laws do not seem to address the current situation directly. Whoever is to challenge the decision to cancel the first term must therefore build a case on other events, which then must be linked to relevant points in the legislation.

A Pleasant Lunch

"This is what is important! This is what I'm passionate about!"

Klaveness is on the phone from Georgia. The Norwegian men's national team has lost 3-0 away to Spain in the Euro 2024 qualifiers and is now in Georgia to play the second game. Klaveness finishes a couple of presidential meetings on the trip.

"I met the Spanish president, Luis Rubiales," she says. "He sits on the UEFA board and is up for re-election."

In other words, the board, called ExCo, the club Klaveness herself wants to be elected to during the UEFA Congress in April.

"There is a very strong culture saying that those who are up for re-election are to be elected. As with all the presidents, I've put forward the issues I believe in, where I can contribute to the ExCo. So, I hope they can support me.

"It was very nice; Rubiales is an open man. He comes from football, so there is a lot of talk about football. Not down to tactics and 4-4-2 versus 4-3-3, but about a new national team coach and things like that. There are a lot of interesting things happening in Spain. Big conflicts, but it is also the country where women's football is growing the most. I can't say whether he will vote for me. But it was rewarding, he is a president you get energy from," she says.

Price from the Conservatives

Rubiales played for Spanish top team Real Betis. Levan Kobiashvili, the president of Georgia, is a legend both in Schalke 04 and in Georgian national football. At the time of Norway's visit to Georgia, a little political drama arose when the Norwegian Conservative Party gave a human rights award to Georgia's former prime minister Mikheil Saakashvili. He is now in custody, and the current prime minister responded by saying that this would be like Georgia giving a similar award to Anders Behring Breivik—the right-wing extremist who killed 77 Norwegians, most of them youth politicians from the Labour Party, in a terrorist attack in 2011.

"And the prime minister is the boss of Kobiashvili."

"Ah, they have the Lukashenko model? The head of the country is the boss everywhere?"

"That model, yes. And Kobiashvili is both football president and parliamentarian," says Klaveness.

She concludes that this meeting was also positive. In other words, she is considerably more satisfied with politics than with football, since Norway ended up playing a 1-1 draw against Georgia. Klaveness says a lot about the two games, but I'm more concerned with the upcoming UEFA election campaign.

Has she made a full circle, and talked to all the national federations?

No.

Are these meetings only about begging for votes?

Not at all, it is a question of microscopic anthropological studies, according to Klaveness: what causes some countries to have older presidents, and thus to be conservative, while others have young leaders and are more progressive? Why are basketball and volleyball bigger than football in Lithuania? What does it mean that the Norwegian state-owned oil company Equinor is heavily present in Azerbaijan? Why is it incomprehensible to some major football countries that Klaveness is running for ExCo after only one year as president? And that she opts for one of the 'open' seats, not the singular one that is reserved for women?

"The custom is that you [need to] be around for many years before you even consider standing for election. And that women struggle against each other for that one woman's seat," she says.

When it comes to the composition of the ExCo, geographical balance has traditionally been the most important thing. It's regional, as Klaveness said. And also, small countries must stand together, and regions such as the Nordic region must rally around one candidate.

"I strongly challenge that. I am more concerned with the gender balance at this moment, there are so few people in the business with knowledge of the women's part of football that this needs priority. We run a business that is divided into girls and boys due to biological differences. It is the world's biggest sport for both. One side is not represented at all. I don't think I will be elected. But I have to tell people now you potentially choose to vote no to the first woman in the ExCo because you are so concerned with geographical balance."

Lisbon, Early April

Two days before the UEFA Congress, and one day before the awarding of the European Championship 2025 is to take place, the photographer and I meet Klaveness in a cafe outside the congress hotel in Lisbon. In advance,

I've tried to find out what the other candidates stand for. Klaveness gives interviews everywhere: Forbes, Sky Sports, Reuters, Ekstra Bladet, and many more, including every major outlet in Norway. No one else does anything like it. In fact, none of them talk to the press at all.

"No, according to the customs, the candidates do not speak to the press. Neither international press nor domestic media. There is also no culture for open discussions about the issues you think are important."

"Then it also means that you don't need to be in the press to win. So, why are you still doing it?"

"Firstly, we want to be an accessible federation, and I want to be an accessible president. So, we have put in extra effort now, because we believe that there is a need for change, and then we have to talk to more people than just football managers. One of the things we want is to create greater transparency around the election process. You notice how closed everything is. We need to talk more openly, in order to find out who you vote for, how power is distributed and how the organisation is run. And secondly, if you are going to have change on these important issues, then there must also be a critical mass that also wants change, and you will not find that among the other presidents. It has to be a movement, quite simply.

"What determines who you will vote for you?"

"In any case, you cannot vote solely for the ones you have a good relationship with. It should be linked to quality and qualifications. I have met most of the candidates who are standing for election. And then I ask what they are interested in."

"Many have promised they'll vote for you. But what you say in one-to-one meetings doesn't necessarily have to have that much weight, when there isn't an open conversation anywhere?

"No, that's exactly the case. Obviously, most people keep their promises. It means a lot to be able to have a private room, and I also do not repeat anything from such conversations when I meet the press. It is important that you know that you can trust each other. One thing is the controlling part, but another thing is ... what can I say, the receptions you get on your reflections," says Klaveness.

Her own reflections are well received by the press, but behind the curtains at UEFA and FIFA, it is more up and down. We enter the UEFA hotel where

Klaveness is doing a half-hour interview with the Dutch national broadcaster. When the microphones are switched off, the Dutch journalists talk about a point of view that is circulating—Lise appears too activist. Klaveness's response: "who says so? Who? WHO?"

But she doesn't get an answer and has to move on to the next meeting. In two hours, the FIFA dinner begins, and in those hours five to six federations are on her meeting list, including the Balkans and the Baltics once again.

Other candidates work differently. Liechtenstein's football president Hugo Quaderer, who is also up for election to the UEFA board, sits in the hotel bar. He is surrounded by seven to eight other men in suits. One of them is Hungarian Sandor Csányi, banker, billionaire and vice-president of the UEFA board. The drinks are brought to the table non-stop; the glasses are emptied and the atmosphere is good. At the other end of the bar sits former stars Luis Figo and Robbie Keane, both caught up in the UEFA system for a long time. Csyáni stops by them, while Quaderer—who due to a "tight schedule" declines to give me an interview during the congress—smiles and toasts to the right and left.

The next day, UEFA's committees have their meetings: the committee for gender and equality rights, the financial committee. Klaveness uses the morning to work her way down her own list. Will she reach her goal of speaking to all of UEFA's 55 member states before the election? Malta's football president Bjorn Vassallo is also a candidate for the UEFA board. He keeps a slower pace than Klaveness and strolls smilingly around the lobby on his own. I decide to ask him some questions.

"If you are elected, what are the cases you're going to work for?"

"UEFA has 55 member countries with many different interests. We have to respect that, and then we have to be aligned with the strategic positions of UEFA. There is always room for improvement, but it must come through discussions, and all stakeholders must be part of the solution."

"Who are these stakeholders?"

"Sponsors. Fans. Media. There are many people in the football industry."

"Precisely, and for supporters and everyone outside the confederations it is impossible to find out what UEFA is discussing, because everything happens behind closed doors, in secrecy?"

"There must be a balance. Things happen in various committees, there is a new working group right now that is going through UEFA's strategic work for the future. Čeferin discusses various federations and tournaments. You can come up with an agenda, which may not be in everyone's interest, but in the end you have to find a common consensus, which is that football brings the change, the positivity, the power and the force that can influence society."

"How do you run your campaign?"

"Through commitment. Conversations. Networking. I have been in UEFA for 15 years, I know people," says Vassallo.

The UEFA ExCo has a meeting from 1 p.m. The main purpose is to decide who gets the women's European Championships in 2025. Sixteen of the board members are entitled to vote. For the first time, there are four applicants for the Euros: France, Switzerland, Poland and the Nordic countries. In the past, it was difficult even to find anyone who wanted to host the championship at all. As recently as 2020, there was only one applicant (England). At the meeting, the board members are given small catalogues that present the various bids. In addition, each applicant has five minutes to present their bid. Then the ExCo casts its secret votes. Everything happens behind closed doors. There is no press conference afterwards for the board members to explain their decision.

UEFA's original plan was to send out the result in a press release, but this was gradually upgraded to be a strictly guarded session with the press. Klaveness is present. Denmark's president Jesper Møller finally ends up next to her—if he still hasn't replied to her text messages, they can at least exchange a few words now. The other bidding federations are also there, as well as a couple of dozen journalists. Then Alexandr Čeferin enters the stage. He says it was a close race. They needed three rounds of voting to get a winner. He opens the envelope ... and the winner is Switzerland. Jesper Møller resolutely gets up from his chair and disappears out of the room and further down the hall, without answering me or the others who call for him to give an interview. Lise Klaveness and Sweden's new football president, Fredrik Reinfeldt, who is a former prime minister from the conservative party Moderaterna, take on the job of talking to the press about the defeat.

In the buzz, it comes out that Switzerland spent half of its five minutes on a rap song performed by a 17-year-old girl. The Nordic countries provided a

PowerPoint presentation and a film. According to the grapevine, certain ExCo members almost proudly expressed that they had not bothered to read the various catalogues. Unlike before, Klaveness now expresses a certain exhaustion.

"I'm just disappointed, really depressed," she says.

Reinfeldt explains the defeat. "There were three rounds of voting, it was close. There is fierce competition; many will want to make their mark in women's football. I am convinced that we are in a general upswing for women's football in the Nordics and Europe."

"*You come from the ordinary political world. How would you describe the meeting with the football democracy?*"

"As you heard, Čeferin emphasised that the democratic principles have been followed, and held firmly to the standard that countries that have applicants were not allowed to vote. I am very confident that democracy is well rooted, and that we have natural working methods here in Europe, even though we know that it is not entirely like that world."

"*Does that also apply to the board election tomorrow?*"

"Yes, in the sense that there are more candidates than there are places, and that each country has its own vote."

"But Čeferin must also be elected. He has no opponents. Neither did Infantino at the FIFA Congress, or Sheikh Salman Al Khalifa at the Asian Football Confederation?"

"No, it is true."

"*You used this point as an argument that football democracy is well functioning?*"

"Yes, well, in these contexts, I don't think that democracy requires more candidates in all cases."

"*Most of the candidates do not speak to the press at all. We have no idea what they stand for. What about Sweden, on what grounds do you choose who to vote for?*"

"An assessment of the efforts they have made, who you know, what they want and stand for ... as you understand, I am new here, that is what I can say about this now," concludes Reinfeldt, while the Swiss toast with champagne to the side. The 17-year-old rap artist was a perfect match for the men in ExCo. The Nordic PowerPoint presentation fell through.

I have an appointment with Switzerland's football president Dominique Blanc. We start to talk about the last European Championship where Switzerland was on the verge of advancing from the group stage.

"*Will they make it in 2025, with home advantage?*"

"Let's hope so, but it will not happen automatically. We see enormous growth in women's football in Switzerland, but we are not alone, so the competition will be fierce," says Switzerland's football president Dominique Blanc.

"*How are the attendances in the top division in Switzerland?*"

"Eh ... I don't have those numbers in my head, but there are 16 teams at the top level, and anyway, we will play each game to win."

"*Tomorrow is the UEFA elections. What distinguishes Lise Klaveness's candidacy from others?*"

"What I see and hear about her from other associations is quite positive. She has strong values, we in Switzerland share them."

"*Switzerland supports her, you only hear positive things. That should mean that the speech she gave in Qatar last year was not particularly controversial. But it is. Why?*"

"She took the risk of giving the speech, alone, where she showed that she stood up for her values. It was a shock to the FIFA members. Suddenly she was a face for this all over the world," says Blanc.

Next there is the UEFA dinner at a restaurant in town. Klaveness's advisor Magnus Borgen has been invited to a party in the hotel bar afterwards— either a celebration or a wake, said the invitation, which went out before the ExCo vote. And in any case, the party will mark the end of the 'Project Lise into ExCo 2023' campaign. But when the FIFA buses return from dinner, no one goes to the bar. Instead, everyone goes to the backyard, and the Norwegian party seems to be cancelled. Lise's entourage also moves, and the invitation is cancelled. Borgen throws up his arms—there are votes to collect, still four or five to go, and Andorra and San Marino await. Through a wall of green garden plants, we see Lise circulating from table to table with men in suits everywhere; she distributes hugs and handshakes to the left and right, then gets down on her knees for a little chat beside someone's chair, before Borgen leads TV2's two reporters into the warmth of UEFA on the last night before the 2023 congress starts.

Election Day

"There's only one left. Bosnia," says Lise at 08:17 the next day as she gets off the UEFA bus on her way into the congress hall.

"Feels good to be finished?"

"At least it's good to know that you've done everything you can. We know the chances of getting elected are very small, but we want to contribute to change, and then we have to talk to everyone, face to face," she says.

Portugal's prime minister António Costa enters the podium first. "Dear Alexander Čeferin, dear Gianni Infantino," he begins. Furthermore, he states that we live in a difficult time, with war in Europe. "Football is a tool for peace, the role of UEFA and everyone is fundamental on the road to peace." But he does not mention that the war against Ukraine actually started during the Olympics in Sochi in 2014, and that it was well underway during the World Cup in Russia in 2018. At that time, Infantino said, on behalf of all the people and organisations he represents, including the Norwegian Football Federation and everyone else in the room, "We all fell in love with Russia." Vladimir Putin replied, "We are all on one big team." And the football world cheered.

Portugal's football president is next; he will say goodbye to UEFA's board to join FIFA but remembers back to when he was first elected. Then, immediately after launching his candidacy, Čeferin was the first to pledge support. "I'll never forget that, Alexandre," he says. Then Infantino gives a speech, and finally Čeferin. For most of his speech he is hammering the Super League—the initiative where the richest clubs in the world tried to create their own league outside the national league systems and UEFA. According to Čeferin, the battle between the Super League and UEFA also represents a number of other contemporary issues: cynicism versus morality, greed versus solidarity, cartels versus meritocracy and democracy, self-absorption versus openness, egoism versus altruism, shameful lies versus the truth, the wolf versus Little Red Riding Hood. If anyone is confused, UEFA stood for the latter word in these pairs of terms in Čeferin's speech.

Along the way, an SMS arrives with a reply to an interview request I sent a few days ago to Jesper Møller. He's going to hold a press conference on the Teams app at 3 p.m. That is immediately after Čeferin's press conference, which will be held immediately after the congress itself. The journalists who want to talk to Møller will have to be quick.

After a couple of hours that mainly consist of a roll call and the approval of various reports, the moment finally arrives. It's election time. First, Čeferin is elected via acclamation. Then Laura McAllister, who is the sole candidate for the sole seat reserved for women, is elected in the same way. Next, the seven new members of the ExCo will be elected, and it will happen in the analog way. In groups of four, the presidents go forward and tick off the names of their preferred candidates on a form. Everyone has seven votes. They can vote for seven different candidates. But they can also choose to just vote for one. When everyone is finished, a six-person team sets about the task of counting the votes. It takes about half an hour. The results are:

Armand Duka (Albania)	45
Jesper Møller (Denmark)	42
Petr Fousek (Czech Republic)	40
Levan Kobiashvili (Georgia)	40
Luis Rubiales (Spain)	40
Philippe Diallo (France)	37
Andriy Pavelko (Ukraine)	31

These seven men were elected to the ExCo, while the next four must wait:

Hugo Quaderer (Liechtenstein)	27
Bjorn Vassallo (Malta)	25
Lise Klaveness (Norway)	18
Rob Petrie (Scotland)	13

In other words, no revolution this time. When the congress is over, Klaveness marches out with a stern look. Outside, she does the rounds with the press, once again alone, without other presidents around her. She talks to the Norwegian, Danish, German, English and Dutch press. First in a joint, impromptu press conference, and then she talks to different outlets one by one. She thanks her team in the NFF, her family and everyone who has supported her, from little girls to soccer mums around Norway.

"No one worked harder than us, I am absolutely sure about that. We will continue to fight. So, it won't be another 100 years where only one of 20 in the management group of the world's largest women's sport is a woman who has knowledge about the women's game. Now the election campaign towards 2025 begins," she says, referring to the next time there will be changes in the ExCo board.

Andreas Selliaas, journalist from the Norwegian sporting and politics news outlet Idrettspolitikk.no, asks if many people had promised to vote for her, but ended up refusing to give her their vote.

"Maybe take away a third of what was promised?" she replies.

I ask, *"wouldn't it be good to be able to trust people? For example, in open voting rounds, where you show who you are voting for?"*

"In general, it is good to be able to trust people. But having secret elections is an important democratic principle. Open elections are good when it comes to the question of trust, but it has some other side effects that are negative. Democracies have experienced this longer than I have been around," says Klaveness.

She keeps it going until Čeferin's press conference begins, and then a message arrives: Jesper Møller's Teams App press conference has been brought forward by half an hour. The photographer and I must drop Čeferin and move to Møller's digital press conference. The Danish football president says the same as Klaveness about open elections. They do not belong in real democracies. On the contrary, all traditions show that in *real* democracies, like the ones in UEFA and FIFA, the elections are secret.

But both Klaveness and Møller forget that in real democracies, there is a principle of distribution of power where different governing institutions control each other. Something like that does not exist in football. In addition, Klaveness and Møller's ideal democracies have external, independent legal entities—in football, such entities are always under UEFA and FIFA themselves in the form of the ethics committees. Politicians in real democracies are obliged to talk to the press. Møller failed to respond to all inquiries before the election, and at the UEFA hotel he has run from one closed UEFA zone to the other, and it is not easy for the journalists to participate in this digital Teams' conference either.

Møller is asked why he never responded to the messages and invitations from Klaveness—he shakes his head and replies that there must be a misunderstanding. He is asked about which issues he will fight for in the next four years—the same as in the previous four is his answer. And he is finally asked why Klaveness was not elected—it showcases that the delegates want geographical diversity on the board.

"You recently stated to DFU's [the Danish Football Union's] own website that the gender balance in football in Denmark is not good enough, that this is something you want to improve and that quotas may be necessary. Do you plan to work for the same in UEFA?"

"We are already doing that," he says.

Quite right, after all, one of the 20 board seats is reserved for a woman!

"We always work to increase the proportion of women, and to improve the conditions for women's football."

"*Then it must have been frustrating that Klaveness was not elected?*"

"We always support our Nordic friends. But people vote the way they do, that's not something we can change," he says.

A couple of hours later at the airport, Klaveness's energy seems to have returned. The airline she's flying with has had some trouble with the online check-in, so the queues are long. 'Camp Klaveness' ends up behind me and the photographer in the line. She talks interchangeably about the upcoming Easter holidays, the UEFA elections and the top division for women's football in Norway: Toppserien. And she expresses some irritation at the punctuation in a novel by Annie Ernaux, which she read on the plane down. And not least, she talks about the procedure for getting onto the UEFA board at the next crossroads, the 2025 congress. Blocs and alliances must be uncovered. And she speculates about the possibilities of a Nordic bid for the women's Euro in 2029.

Pink Shoes

A week has passed. Klaveness has been debriefed after Portugal, and she has been in the biggest city in southern Norway, Kristiansand, to talk to the women's team of Start, one of the more traditional clubs in Norwegian top football. She's also visited the federation of Agder, which is the county of Start and the rest of the Norwegian south.

But now, on a sunny April Tuesday morning, she is standing at the Linderud football pitch in Eastern Oslo. It lies just below the legendary subway line 5, which over the years gathered an undeserved 'heart of darkness'-like reputation. The line goes into the Grorud Valley—the most multicultural part of the Norwegian capital, and the concrete walls in the area have always been more colourful than in any other part of town due to graffiti artists working there over the years. The pitch is surrounded by blocks, and hundreds of girls from the lowest grades of elementary schools in the area are gathered on the artificial grass pitch. Schools like Ellingsrud, Stovner, Haugen, Årvoll, Trosterud, Vestli and so on.

"The Pink Shoes project was started by Eli Landsem, our teacher," says Bina Ahmadi, who plays on Grorud's senior team and is in her last year on the three-year sports program at Bjerke High School. Eli Landsem started working there as a teacher not long after she quit as national team manager in 2012. She assembled a working group to find out how to increase football participation among minority girls. Klaveness was part of this group.

"The girls from the third grade take full responsibility for the arrangement, and we started our work right after the summer holidays," Ahmadi continues, while Klaveness applauds as the girls march into the sports hall next to the pitch, one school after another. Finally, Landsem herself arrives, and she does a trademark Ronaldo celebration in front of a group of boys aged 18-19 who are part of the Pink Shoes team. The guys respond with today's loudest cheer in honour of Landsem.

Once inside, the girls are welcomed by Ahmadi and her friend and colleague, Nawail Butt. The duo launches a super day filled with football, dancing and a barbecue, before handing the microphone to today's guest of honour.

"It's so nice that all of you came to my birthday," says Klaveness, who turns 42 today. She talks about the ball that was always with her when she was a little girl. In other words, the old story from her Qatar speech, and continues to present three pieces of advice to the girls at Linderud.

"One: get to know your team, create a good environment, have fun, don't listen to those who say you have to train because it's important. Have fun instead. Two: dare to try things you can't. Three: and this is the most important thing—dare to lose, dare to screw up. The toughest are those who dare to make mistakes and go on to try again and again. And if any one of you wonder about anything, or need tips and inspiration or whatever, get in touch. Call someone in the NFF, they'll give you my phone number or email. If you contact me I'll answer you."

Then Ahmadi and Butt lead the girls in the hall through the birthday song. Then, of course, it's time for the so-called 'Bli med-dans', which translates from Norwegian to English as 'The Come and Join Dance', a groovy song and dance that is performed at all the schools in Norway on various occasions throughout the year. Today Ahmadi and Butt sing and dance with the primary school girls in front of them, and also the youths from the sports classes at Bjerke High School, including the football boys in their late teens.

"It is part of the sports management course. We've been out to different schools in this area, we've been teaching the children for a month, and played football with them, and this is the big day, when they all come out here," says Butt, whose main sport is dance, but who plays football on the day.

"To get the children into football, they need to see girls who are older, who are involved and engage them, and are role models. Then they will join. I remember even when I was little and played football in Grorud, there was no one I could look up to who could be there and say, 'hey, come and play football!' It was more like I did it completely independently," says Ahmadi.

"The aim of the whole project is to get more girls to choose football. We start by saying we are a bit cooler than the boys; we dare to take the ball from them in the schoolyard," says Butt.

Then the games begin. They've divided the artificial turf into 12 small courts. And the girls run, dribble, shoot, score, tackle, cheer and cry.

"Lisbon was emotionally hard. This is just fun," says Klaveness about the variety of work tasks as football president. "The question is how we can make all these girls become club members and proper players," she says, still in work mode.

As with the rest of football in Norway, not all clubs in Oslo East have anything to offer potential girl players. Many clubs lack senior teams, clubs have to merge, and the trips to and from training become too long, too soon. However, Romsås IL is an exception.

"I spoke to several of the girls, and they said they only played football at school. This is a very nice entrance door, but we have to get them on board properly," says Klaveness. She talks about how the NFF can get involved with the young girls from the area and the county federation, how the girls and the Pink Shoes project can become part of the work and structure of Norwegian football, and of course, how things can get 'operationalised'— probably the word Lise Klaveness uses most often—but between the blocks at Linderud, it is unclear to me what is about to be operationalised in this context.

"We need to get a proper dialogue going with Eli Landsem," says Klaveness, before starting a meeting with Landsem out on the pitch. The culture minister from the Labour Party, Anette Trettebergstuen, shows up dressed in a suit. She stops by for ten minutes, enough to take a selfie with Lise before turning around in her high heels and leaving in her black car. Kamzy Gunaratnam, another Labour politician, was also at the scene, as was Norwegian sports president Berit Kjøll, assistant coach of the women's national team Monica Knudsen and an old football man: veteran striker Ibba Lajaab, who currently plays for Lyn at level four, and who also works at one of the schools in Eastern Oslo.

"On days like this, there must be a bit of real content too," says Klaveness. "I'm not too fond of events that are only ceremonial."

Røa, Oslo West, May 6

Spring is in full bloom for football players of all ages in Norway. A week-and-a-half after the event in Oslo East, Klaveness is on another artificial turf pitch, now in Oslo West. But here there are no blocks in sight. Only nice and tidy detached houses and well-kept gardens. Grey-haired pensioners cut the roses, while the family houses have a barbecue on the veranda and a trampoline on the lawn. We are at Røa. It's a neighbourhood with a view towards Holmenkollen, one of the most expensive parts of Oslo to live in with its famous ski jump hill on top of the residential area.

Røa has been a top team in women's football for 25 years. It's a small club with the men's team competing in the seventh tier, and the stadium capacity is 450. The women's team has won the series and the cup five times each, played in the Champions League and, since promotion in 1999, has only had one season-long trip down to the second tier.

Unlike Bina Ahmadi, the young girls in this rich area have always had role models to look up to. There's never been any reason to change clubs because the girls' team disappeared, as Ahmadi had to. And Røa is not the only top team in Oslo West. Lyn and Stabæk are two others. The eastern edge only has Vålerenga, close to the centre, which still clings to a kind of working-class image, even though the core neighbourhood for the club in 2023 is largely middle-class through districts such as Kampen and Etterstad.

Today, there is a match between Røa and Brann, who won the league and cup double last year. In 2023 they are both mid-table, with Brann a couple of points above Røa. Klaveness played 73 games for Norway, she won league and cup golds for clubs in Sweden and Norway—and she also played for Sandviken, the team that before last season became Brann, and suddenly is getting one of Norway's loudest supporter groups on their side. But Klaveness is not at the Røa Stadium to cheer. She is here to present an award: *ildsjel* of the day—in English it translates to something like *super volunteer* of the day.

Each time Klaveness attends a game in the men's or women's top flight this year, she will carry a national team kit with *ildsjel* written on the back. Even the top teams need someone to make waffles, and at Røa it is Harald Nickelsen who has been mixing eggs and milk for a short lifetime. And maybe a little extra sugar. Klaveness brags about "the famous Røa waffles" in her speech, which is held during the break. She talks about Nickelsen's career on Røa's senior team, her own embarrassing losses on this very pitch when she was a player herself, and about the general importance of driving forces like Nickelsen, who leave behind hundreds of work hours, and even more heart and soul, all for free, behind the scenes of the top teams.

The second half begins, and after Brann's dominance in the first, Røa is now on fire. Ten minutes into the second half, Tuva Espås scored in a counterattack to make it 1–0. Brann equalises a few minutes later.

"No, it's not possible," says Klaveness when asked if it is appropriate to cheer when Brann scores.

She is surrounded by old Røa faces with a lot of feelings for the club. And Røa's future is uncertain—a relevant question is whether such a small club should even have a place in the future of top football in Norway.

"When I'm at Røa, I think, damn it, so little has happened regarding professionalism for top football for women in Norway. Røa are unique in Norwegian history in the way they climbed from the lower divisions into a position where they for a period won everything. But what remains is that such a story creates higher income, through spectators and sponsors, to create a greater sustainability for professionalism for the players," she says.

Not long ago, national broadcaster NRK published a story about players from the top tier still having to have a job in addition to playing football, with Røa's goalkeeper being an example. She is also a kindergarten teacher.

"It is the same system here now as it was when I played. Ten years ago, the stadium was also bad. It is impressive that Røa still manages to be a top club. That the chairman, who has to deal with lots of complex legal issues, is also the one who makes the waffles," says Klaveness.

"When we applied for the Euro, there were a couple of things that the Euro should be used for. One of them was to professionalise the top tier, another was to make football a better arena for inclusion of girls," she says.

The municipality of Oslo wanted to invest 26 million, but even if the European Championship went to Switzerland, the goals from the NFF are the same. They're going to send a new application to the municipality for support for a project for the inclusion of minority girls.

"The essence of what we are looking for is simply to expand Pink Shoes to make it bigger," says Klaveness.

Then Røa scores again and the match ends at 2-1. But Klaveness has entered the artificial grass behind Røa's goal. There she's playing football and chatting with the children. Tips and experiences are exchanged between selfies and autographs. Klaveness is asking all kinds of questions, like what motivates the children, who do they cheer for, what do they like to do most? She has brought her wife and the couple's three children to the match, and after 90 minutes of football, they are ready for the evening. In the end, the football president manages to break free from the playful scene behind the goal, and their Volvo five-seater is filled up and then finds its way among the roses and trampolines before heading home.

Finland

There are Pink Shoes in Finland too. In early May, Klaveness visits Norway's neighbouring country for the 50th anniversary of Finnish women's football. The NFF president was to give a speech in front of the pioneers and had prepared a PowerPoint that was about the obvious things: women and football.

"But when I'm on stage, another PowerPoint appears. A presentation I gave for the Oslo Business Forum a little earlier. And I realise, while I'm on stage, that I can't get it changed, it's impossible to retrieve the presentation that should actually be there. Totally, totally terrible," says Klaveness a couple of days later.

Her solution was to pretend it was all natural.

"I ended up giving the same presentation that I had for [the] Oslo Business Forum. About management and organisation, with pictures of Erling Braut Haaland and Ståle Solbakken and guys like that. Zero focus on gender equality. Way too few women in the pictures. Only management. But nobody said anything."

Ullevaal, May 8

"We from the government are big fans of championships," says state secretary Gry Haugsbakken from the Ministry of Culture (KUD). She is sitting on a stage at Ullevaal, and under a cloth in a room nearby is the World Cup trophy. The World Cup is getting close, and Norway will play the opening match against New Zealand on July 20 in Auckland at 8 p.m. local time. As always, the trophy is on a world tour. With a bunch of companions from FIFA, the trip started in Japan, took a roundabout in Asia, onwards to Africa, across the Atlantic to Brazil and the rest of South America, via the Caribbean to the USA, across the Atlantic again and to Europe, before Australia and New Zealand awaits at the end. On Norway's Liberation Day, the trophy has arrived in Oslo, and the day starts with a seminar.

The first item on the agenda is the Ministry of Culture's thoughts on championships and equality. Klaveness receives a solid dose of praise from Haugsbakken, but the state secretary also emphasises that "she needs help from all of you". It seems as if she wants to limit a supposed underlying expectation that the football president will perform miracles on her own.

After Haugsbakken, representatives from the embassies of New Zealand enter the stage, together with two former Matildas: Alison Leigh Forman and Alicia Ferguson-Cook. It's time for nostalgia and memories because when these ladies played on the Australian national team, they had several tough encounters with another person in the room—Hege Riise, Norwegian national team coach, who became a world champion and was elected the tournament's best player in 1995.

Forman talks about how far ahead Scandinavia was when she travelled from Australia to Denmark to play in the 1990s. Everyone knows that in 2023, Norway has fallen behind, while clubs like Real Madrid and Arsenal, who barely had a women's team back then, sell out their biggest arenas for important matches. Then Karl-Petter Løken takes over, the secretary general from the NFF, with a strange speech about how good Euro 2025 would have been if the Nordics had won the bid, and not Switzerland. Løken paints such a perfect picture that one suspects the NFF is planning a new application for 2029. Next, we're shown a couple of video clips sent in from Brann, both from the men's and the women's teams. Then, it is time for Klaveness.

As usual, she starts speaking about the ball in her childhood, and today she pauses on one point we remember from Pink Shoes: the lack of role models, which was a problem when Klaveness grew up. For the young, football-juggling Klaveness, the Norwegian national team didn't exist at all. That team was so far below the mainstream radar, even though it was one of the best in the world. Nevertheless, "the strength of the ball brought me in," says Klaveness. But it can't be like that anymore, because if it is, many of the youngest players will disappear. Therefore, the grassroots work must be better structured, and on the screen behind her she shows a manipulated picture of a football stadium where the grass is as steep as an alpine slope. The girls' teams are at the bottom of the hill and the players will face an uphill struggle throughout their careers. For guys, it's the opposite. She points to the two U-17 national team players who will go up on stage after her. If their brothers also play football, in every area, at any point in their careers, they will get a much better offer than their sisters. "How do we address this?" she asks.

Some of the answers: more tickets need to be sold, female coaches and managers must be brought in, the girls must be given something to dream about.

Another elephant, which was avoided by the team who promoted the FIFA World Cup 2023 at today's event, is the current state of some of the world's best national teams. There's been a revolt in France, with four of the biggest stars refusing to play for the national team anymore. In Spain, 15 players have been on strike for a year; it is uncertain whether they will participate in the World Cup. USA's team has taken its union to court, the Nigerian players are fighting to be paid rightful sums from their union, and in Colombia it has recently emerged that financial and sexual exploitation of the players was almost institutionalised.

2020 Olympic winner Canada is on the boil for two reasons. One is that the players are on strike for equal pay and working conditions. The other is due to former U-20 national team coach Bob Birarda, who also coached the biggest club in the country at the time, Vancouver Whitecaps. He was imprisoned in 2022, convicted of sexual abuse of players in the period 1998–2008.

An additional dispute in the case is that he lost his job in the Whitecaps and the U-20 national team in 2008 because the management of Canada Soccer (the football federation of the country) was informed of his activity. Nevertheless, from 2009 to 2019 he was a coach for other women's teams, even though the leaders of Canada Soccer knew that he had abused young girls he coached. One of these leaders is CONCACAF president and FIFA vice-president, Victor Montagliani. Another is Peter Montapoli, who is now head of Canada's World Cup 2026 committee. A third is Norwegian Even Pellerud, who was the coach of Canada's senior team during the same period, who is also a former coach of the Norwegian national team and he now works in the corridors at Ullevaal. When I wrote about this case for *Josimar*, I interviewed Pellerud. He said he reported Birarda's misconduct to his superiors as soon as he heard about it, and that further action from him was beyond his work tasks.[1]

---

[1] The full quotes from Pellerud can be read at https://josimar.no/for-abonnenter/what-was-it-christine-was-bitching-about/20306/

But this is a FIFA event with guests from different continents. It's all about telling the world how good this year's World Cup will be. Finally, the trophy is unveiled by Hege Riise. Perhaps she is wondering, through the flashlights, where her own trophy is. In Norway it's well known, but the embarrassment is so big we prefer not to talk about it with outsiders: we won the World Cup in Sweden in 1995, but the trophy disappeared shortly after the players came home. The football federation didn't look after it properly, and suddenly—Norway's only World Cup trophy was gone, never to be seen again.

"There was another type of person who came up to me today," says Klaveness when the seminar is over.

"For example, the ambassador of Morocco. We're going to find a time to meet again, she had many exciting things to say about young Moroccan girls living in Norway. It's that speech again, she felt it really strongly," Klaveness says.

This response from the Moroccan ambassador illustrates that 'the Arab world' is more than the rich tourists in the fan zones who were interviewed by the Norwegian broadcasters (NRK and TV2) during World Cup 2022, and who all supported Infantino's narrative.

The Faroe Islands

From May 11 to 13, Lise Klaveness was in the Faroe Islands, a small archipelago in the North Atlantic, halfway from Norway towards Iceland. The occasion was a meeting between the Nordic football federations. In other words, the countries that cooperated on the Euro application for 2025, but whixh did not cooperate in the application process for places on UEFA's board.

"There was an atmosphere in the Faroe Islands, no doubt. It was tough," says Klaveness.

Let's return to the UEFA Congress in Lisbon, and the press conferences afterwards. Jesper Møller said that the Nordic collaboration worked out fine, it was only Klaveness who had "misunderstood" a few things. Klaveness also claimed that the Nordic cooperation went well.

"In the Faroe Islands, it was highlighted that Nordic cooperation is difficult right now," she says, after firstly saying that the Faroe Islands is a conservative country ("but also a wonderful place", she adds, as if to ensure that no one is offended).

The Faroe Islands are part of Denmark. They have self-government, but also have two representatives in the Danish parliament. Unlike Denmark, the Faroe Islands is not a member of the EU. But the country has its own seat in FIFA and UEFA, and that gives the micro-country with 54,000 inhabitants voting rights with the same weight as giants like Brazil and Germany. In a survey from 2017, 80 percent of the population stated that they have a strong faith in God, and almost 40 percent go to a church service monthly. This indicates that the population is significantly more religious than the rest of the Scandinavian countries.

"They have tough discussions about abortion, LGBTQ, those things. The football president, Christian Andreasen, is a nice guy. He is also a politician and has led this very conservative party," says Klaveness.

The party she is talking about is called Fólkaflokkurin. It is a party with roots in revival Christianity, and it has traditional Christian ethics as a political-ethical guideline.

"They are concerned with keeping politics out of football, but it is difficult on that island, when political issues are discussed within football, since the population is very divided," says Klaveness, and she gives the impression that her candidacy for UEFA ExCo, in combination with her Doha speech, has taken the form of a political statement in the Faroese context.

"Now I got the feeling that the whole Nordic cooperation ended up in a bad light because I ran for election. That's how it was perceived—but it wasn't how it was intended on my part. I thought it was in the best interests of Nordic cooperation. If you want a change, you must dare to take risks. If you don't want change, you can work quietly," she says of the discussions among the 50–60 participants at the meeting in the Faroes.

"This stuff requires a strong back. It's oppressive and uncomfortable because I don't want to ruin things for anyone. I don't want to ruin things for the Nordic countries. The easiest thing to get the mood up would be to just say sorry for everything. To back away. Admit that I shouldn't have done it in the first place," she says.

In other words, they want her to say something completely different from what she said after the congress in Lisbon.

"That is the tight corner we are stuck in now," she says.

"I wanted to speak to Jesper Møller in advance. We didn't manage to do that. The meeting in the Faroe Islands was good in the sense that this issue was discussed. But it is tough because of the special atmosphere that occurs. But what is the actual elephant in the room? It's that we think the need for change is urgent," she says.

After dark, on the windswept islands, Klaveness wants to relax a little after a long day. She has a glass of wine in the hotel bar, sitting together with Annika Grälls, who has worked for women's football in Sweden for many years.

"Then a man comes over and starts shouting at me because I ran for election for the UEFA ExCo. He was drunk and loud. Like when you support a football team ... and are very upset because your team lost. He yelled at me. YOU JUST DON'T DO SUCH A THING," she says, imitating Danish.

"Later I learned that he was not from any boards or federations or anything, he was just an ordinary guy. You don't imagine that. Someone from outside football is coming up to you, giving you the scolding because you believed you could run for office just because you're a woman. That's the way it is right now. It was a special trip. The Faroe Islands is a super cool place, but we didn't know we'd cause such a stir there in that way."

3
SUMMER

Caroline Graham Hansen and Ingrid Syrstad Engen win the Champions League with Barcelona. Erling Braut Haaland wins the Champions League and Premier League with Manchester City.

At home in Norway, new super volunteers are singled out every weekend. Teddy Moen, a man of honour and long-time leader in the football coaches' association, dies of cancer. There's 'walking football' for elders at Manglerud in Oslo East, and 'colourful football' for the children of immigrants at Valle Hovin, a stadium in Oslo East.

Klaveness is on a club visit in the Grorud Valley and attends an event called 'Disney football' at Oslo East with Labour Party politician Kamzy Gunaratman. She also visits training for the national team for people of small stature, and she oversees football events for girls in Bosnia. More super volunteers are singled out. Then it's the Skaugum Cup, on the stately country farm of the royal family, together with Norway's crown prince and crown princess. And last, but not least: the national championship for street teams in Bergen, where Klaveness is elected to the board of the Norwegian street team association.

Everything is documented on Klaveness's never-resting Instagram account. "The street teams really are jewels, when we talk about social sustainability in football and in society. Every time I meet these players, who either have or have had drug problems and are in struggles that are incredibly difficult, I am moved and inspired. Many describe how they've gone from being ashamed and walking around staring at the ground, to feel like proud parts of the local club, and how the team has become a family they longed for," she writes.

Since 2015, 600 people have returned to working life because of the street teams. The benefit to society is calculated to be more than NOK 430 million annually. "There are few projects in the field of drug rehab that can show similar results," she writes.

But there are also examples of top clubs who've taken money originally earmarked for the street teams away from them, and instead used the money on their senior teams.

The Anatomy of a Defeat

In May and June, it becomes clear that the team around Klaveness has made up their minds about how this project—i.e., this text, the book you are now reading—should end up. Yes, the NFF practises full transparency, and Klaveness answers questions when the media ask. In this case, she agreed to an annual reporting project, a kind of anthropological journalism, where participatory observation was to be the main element. But there are many indications that the group behind her primarily wants Klaveness to be seen as a good Samaritan: as a leader of the street team foundation, a fighter for the rights of Muslim girls from the poor parts of town, and an ambassador for Norwegian values among girl players in the Balkans. We are invited to such events two, three and four times. But when we ask for a chat around the time of the two national team matches in June, where we could also talk properly about the results in the first six months, the requests are left unanswered in classic NFF/FIFA/UEFA style.

Norway will face Scotland on June 17, and then Cyprus three days later. With only one point from the first two Euro 2024 qualifiers, we must win both the games in June to have any chance to make it to the Euro. It's summer, it's sunny and warm, and Ullevaal Stadium is sold out. Everything is the way it should be, and it all starts well against Scotland. Norway controls the game, and Erling Braut Haaland scores after about an hour. We seem to stroll comfortably on to three points, but out of nowhere, the Norwegian defence serves the ball to Scotland's striker. It's three minutes before the end, and it's 1–1. Exactly the same thing happened against Georgia, when we gave them the ball towards the end. Two minutes later, Scotland scores again. Inexplicably, we have given away the victory.

I continue to try to nail down a football talk with Klaveness, and at the last minute I get an invitation to the press conference after the NFF president has met Norway's prime minister Jonas Gahr Støre from the Labour Party. The meeting is scheduled for 20:15, i.e., 30 minutes before the match against Cyprus begins. During these 30 minutes, Lise and Jonas will each give their own introduction, and 8–10 media outlets will be allowed to ask their questions—and everyone must make it to the 8.45 p.m. kick-off.

"It's a good atmosphere in there," says the NFF's media person, nodding in the direction of Støre and Klaveness, when she announces the duo's arrival a few minutes before time. When the session finally starts, we're already a couple of minutes late.

Klaveness hammers the EU's recent rubber granulate ban. The prime minister's colleagues in the Labour Party-run Oslo City Council have also adopted a ban on rubber granules. The duo agrees that Norway must take the lead in work to find good solutions. Much like taking the lead in the difficult work of transitioning to renewable energy. "We are not against the ban," says Klaveness, in the same way that Støre is not against slowing down oil production. But in a related manner, Klaveness doesn't want to rush to end the rubber granule era, and Støre doesn't want to rush to end the oil era.

Everyone is busy at the meeting—because no one wants to be there. We all want to go to the match afterwards, and no one is allowed to ask more than one question. This means that there will be few critical granule questions to answer for the duo.

Afterwards, Cyprus is waiting on the pitch. Norway wins 3–1, and finally manages to secure three points.

Euro for the Young

Shortly afterwards, Klaveness goes to Romania to watch Norway's men's U-21 team who are participating in the Euro. The trip to Cluj turns out to be arduous, with cancelled flights and full airports. The president's journey took more than one day each way. Normally, the trip should take five hours. Finally, we can talk over the phone after Norway has lost 2–1 against Switzerland in the opening match. Italy and France are the next opponents.

"*How would you summarise the first half of the year? Out on the pitch,*

I guess it hasn't gone quite as planned?"

"It's not about things not going as planned, because football life never goes as planned. For the first time in 10 years, we are in the U-21 Euros; that is very good. We were better than Switzerland. It's not the result that counts in this age group, it's the performance. Nothing more. What we want for the players is to learn to be in championships. It's always hard to lose, which I also do on behalf of the boys. But it's a victory just to be there. As a president of the NFF, my job is only to think long term. It's to see the bigger picture. But the singular match performances, that's for the national team manager to think about."

"Norway has qualified in quite a few championships for age-specific national teams. But this has in no way manifested itself in better results for the senior national team. This indicates that something is wrong with the way we work with age-specific national teams in Norway?"

"That is a big question. First, we haven't been *that* good in the years past. We qualified for U-21 Euros this year, and that was for the first time in many years. U-19 qualified a few years ago, at the time they hadn't done it for a long time, but then they have qualified every time since. It is fantastically good for a small country like Norway. But from there on, it hasn't been as good. So, the question is worth asking. The Scotland game was one of the worst I have … apart from 0-8 against England in the Euros last year," she says, about the loss the women's team suffered in a group stage game against the later European champions.

"That was a terrible experience, primarily for empathetic reasons. Another thing is the lost opportunities for the children who are here, here and now, to see Norway in the play-offs."

"We have three Champions League winners this year from Barcelona and Manchester City. We won gold and silver in the Premier League for men. On the women's side, our players have won the league in England, Spain, France, Germany and Italy. But the national teams just can't make it work. Our motto is 'stronger together', but it doesn't seem to be like that with our senior teams, rather we are weaker together?"

"In the 1990s, everything was good in Norwegian football. The men's national team, the women's national team, club football for men, club football for ladies. A general boost, which I personally, and many with me, attribute to the fact that we had some common ideas in Norwegian football, regarding, for example, equal structure and zonal marking. The coaches were academics. They were clever on the training ground but had an academic approach as well. People laughed at Drillo," she says coach Egil "Drillo" Olsen who took Norway to the World Cup in 1994 and 1998, and to an incredible second place on the FIFA rankings.

"But he made people follow him. We were ahead of Europe regarding the analytic work. It's not so easy to be ahead of someone anymore. Football has professionalised a hundredfold. We are adopting a new sports plan in the NFF board now. And the first point in this plan is that we have to be curious ourselves as a board of football and as an entire movement. We must have a culture of sharing and acquiring expertise. Our curiosity must give us a competitive advantage. We have set aside three million dollars a year to obtain data and insight about the game. It's heavy stuff, you won't get results tomorrow."

"So sharing is the main point. But that must have been done before?"

"It has, sharing is part of Norwegian culture. People generally know technology, know how to analyse, they've educated themselves as coaches for a long time, they share a lot, there is little corruption and people trust each other. If people from another association ask, I share with them. Of course, it has been done before, but we should do it more, faster, better. Spain, Germany and England have 60 people employed in their analysis sections. We have no chance of catching up with anyone in terms of how much innovation you can generate. What I'm talking about is bringing things together across club, gender, and national teams, and making it effective. We need to get a centre for top football. Not necessarily the physical place, but a mentality around working together, every day, all the time. First, through insight and knowledge. We're not going to engage in pub talk. And next, through new national training facilities."

"Such a facility is far into the future, isn't it?"

"Well, we've already done the most important thing. People discuss for 10–15 years, then you decide on a place. After that, it goes quickly."

"You're done with the discussion? But you don't have a specific location yet?"

"No, that's where we are now. It has to be near Ullevaal. There's a place near Gardermoen Airport that is a possibility. Karl-Petter and I are also looking at other places, primarily in Oslo," she says about the secretary general.

"Imagine if we could've done it in Stovner or Grorud Valley," she says about the areas of the city that are most plagued by gangs and criminality, but also home to large numbers of children, many of them from families with lower education and lesser income.

"I saw a grass pitch in that area when we were out visiting clubs with the city council. I ran up to the pitch and looked around. I thought, DAMN—this is where we should have the national training facility. I looked at Karl-Petter and saw that he was thinking exactly the same thing. In terms of integration, it could have been symbolic and nice, and it could have contributed to building a more robust football culture in that area."

"The East End is incredibly far behind the West End in terms of resources?"

"The clubs are struggling with getting enough volunteers. As you can see in Sweden, the clubs disappear and there's more and more crime. A national facility centre there could be very good. It's a little dream, but it's too early to conclude. But we can't throw it out as an idea, and get all the arguments against it, until we've looked at the actual possibilities."

"But before that you have to find out what doesn't work in the transition from age-specific national teams to seniors, as we spoke about?"

"We need insight into the entire pyramid. The children must see that there are opportunities, that they have a chance. We see how we systematically give advantage to children who are developed early. We know that when they are small, they are better than those who are late-developed. It is difficult not to give this kind of advantage, you have to make a conscious effort not to do it. We have set up money to have a 'future national team' on the boys' side."

"That's a kind of national team for young players with late physical development?"

"Yes. There we have an academic approach and select those who are thought to have potential, but whose physical development is slow. There can be a six-year difference in development between children of the same age when they are in their early teens. On the girls' side, it is the opposite. Girls who are late in development are often preferred, because of how the muscles develop differently for boys and girls during puberty. At that stage, girls can get the feeling of stagnation, of getting heavier without the muscles developing at the same pace if they don't exercise in the right way. Many at the youth stage quit, especially girls. About half of them quit, then there are a lot who want to play on, but who have no team to play with, because there is no structure or culture to team up with, for example, the neighbouring club," she says, about the all-too-familiar situation in girls' football where teams have to quit because of a lack of players.

"And on top of the pyramid, the men's national team coach Ståle Solbakken got a new contract, just before these last two qualifying matches?"

"Yes, and when we lost, many asked questions about that. About Ståle's position. But nobody here thinks that we will lose a football match because of Ståle. The board is unanimous in the conclusion that Ståle is the right man for the job, no matter if we qualify for the next Euros or not."

The World Cup in Australia and New Zealand

It's July 19, one day before the World Cup starts. National team manager Hege Riise sits on a podium at Eden Park in Auckland together with Caroline Graham Hansen (Barcelona) and Maren Mjelde (Chelsea). With a stoney face, Graham Hansen says that the atmosphere in the squad is fantastic. Riise says the same. The only person who expresses something close to the same with body language and words is captain Maren Mjelde. Perhaps her good mood comes from the feeling of home she presumably gets because of the cold rain outside the windows—it is reminiscent of the weather in Mjelde's hometown of Bergen in late October.

"I was close. On the way to the gym. Bang, bang, bang. What were those sounds? Then a joint message was sent out to the whole group—everyone's inside, right? Because all the players were inside the hotel. But everyone wasn't inside. I was outside. Actually, it was better. I saw the police come, [and] that he was taken. But some of the players were inside and heard shots from outside. They had someone who actively looked after them. Then you get a little scared."

Klaveness is talking about the shots that rocked New Zealand early in the morning on July 20, the opening day of the World Cup. A 24-year-old man, previously convicted, entrenched himself on a construction site, a few hundred metres from the Norwegian hotel, and began to fire shots at random workers. Three died, and one of them was the 24-year-old himself. The whole of New Zealand mourns as such incidents seldom occur in this peaceful corner of the world.

"How are the World Cup vibes in the Norwegian squad, in rainy, sorrowful New Zealand, in cold wind and 11 degrees, on the day of the first match?"

"It's still good," says Klaveness, a few hours after the shots were fired and we stand by the team bus outside the Norwegian players' hotel. "Strong. The energy in the squad has been very good. It's a dangerous thing to say, and I don't like to say it. But it has. They have plenty of self-confidence," she says.

It's an echo of what Hansen and Riise said at the press conference yesterday. Behind us, the Norwegian players begin to leave the hotel and enter the bus which will take them to Eden Park, Auckland's largest stadium. There are cheers in the lobby for every player that passes. Ada Hegerberg, Emilie Haavi, Tuva Hansen, Guro Reiten and all the others. They are smiling and waving. Safe and confident, and on their way to one of the greatest things a football player can experience, the opening game of a World Cup. With 40,000 in the stands, and on the other half of the pitch, "The Ferns", the New Zealand team who haven't won a World Cup game in 14 attempts. But they may have received an involuntary extra boost—the national tragedy of the shooting episode could be a potentially unifying force for the country.

"We really don't have very good experience of meeting the host nation. We faced the Netherlands in 2017 and were swept off the field. England beat us 8–0 in the previous Euros. Home nations have an extra power."

"New Zealand is not as good as the Netherlands and England?"

"No, and we didn't think the Netherlands were good that year."

"They were very good."

"They were. But New Zealand will not be on that level. I don't think the shooting affects the Norwegian players, even if it's a terrible incident. The training sessions have been good, we are excited," says Klaveness, and now all the players have boarded the bus. They wait for one person, the football president, who gives the victory sign as she enters the bus.

Two hours later, after a wonderful opening ceremony showcasing colourful elements from Maori culture, the match kicks-off. And it immediately becomes clear that the self-confidence that Klaveness talked about has evaporated. Norway looks terrified. Especially defensively. Keeper Aurora Mikalsen (Brann) stays on the line when she could easily go out and interfere with a pass going over the defence line. Left back Tuva Hansen (Bayern Munich) is outrun and dribbled. The two centre backs are constantly hesitating. Defensive midfielder Ingrid Syrstad Engen (Barcelona) loses all duels. Absolutely nothing works. Ada Hegerberg (Lyon) and Caroline Graham Hansen, Norway's superstars in attack, create a couple of chances each on their own. But the interactions between them don't work. Guro Reiten, who had a great season at Chelsea, is completely invisible. It's like watching a replay of the disaster against England at Euro 2022.

New Zealand gains more and more confidence as the minutes go by. When Norway left the hotel, the lobby behind them cheered. The home team has a stadium full of happy Kiwis on fire. It is a rugby nation cheering every time the ball is played forward, every time a tackle or a header is won. It's inevitable, and two minutes into the second half, it happens. The ball is played from the goalkeeper up through the middle of the pitch, then out on the right without Norway even being close to touching it. Next, the ball is passed into the box, and Norway is still lagging. Hannah Wilkinson (Melbourne City) makes no mistake from five yards and the stadium explodes.

After such a setback, you could expect that Norway's star gallery would immediately put massive pressure on the underdogs in black jerseys. This doesn't happen. It is only in the last ten minutes that we manage to create a couple of chances, but still it is the home team who are awarded a penalty a minute before the end. Incredibly, the ball hits the crossbar, and Norway gets an equally incredible nine minutes of added time. But all we get during that time is our own shot at the crossbar. The referee blows after 99 minutes, and the Kiwis storm the pitch. Players and fans alike are dancing and crying in a fantastic football celebration for the home team.

Out on the grass, Ada Hegerberg looks furious. Caroline Graham Hansen is completely knocked out. The Norwegian players form three circles, and only they themselves know what is said. Afterwards, they limp their way to painful sessions at the press conference and mixed zone. Among them, Lise Klaveness.

"It's not for saying specific things, really," she says later. "But to give a high five and say thank you for the match. It's just about offering people a hug, because it's really tough to lose the opening game. It's about standing together with the team when we lose, as a kind of care. When you're a player in such a situation, you like to think that what you experienced is unique, that nothing worked, you are angry and sad. Then I have to pull out all the other opening games that we have lost. Like at the Olympics in Sydney 2000, when we won in the end. For me, it's about reading the room. Try to figure out if there's anyone you can talk to. But it is the coach's role to step in and have the detailed conversations," she says.

"It will also go down in history that New Zealand played a fantastic game."

"Absolutely. They have been training together as a club team for three or four months. The shooting drama made the whole game a larger-than-life feeling. They are playing at home for the first time, because this team never plays at home, really. It's because of club football and the large distances. They are a mediocre team that was transformed into a superpower," says Klaveness.

"She's like Pippi Longstocking!"

It is the Norwegian ambassador in New Zealand, Anne Grete Riise, who says this about Klaveness, the day after the opening match.

Pippi Longstocking is a fictional character from the children's books of Swedish author Astrid Lindgren, and a common reference in Nordic countries. The ginger-haired, freckled Pippi is 9–10 years old and lives alone, as her father is a pirate and always out sailing. She's a super-strong rebel, able to outsmart the police and kick around even the most threatening thieves. She can carry a horse with one arm and is always full of self-confidence. The ambassador goes on to reproduce Pippi's most famous quote: "I've never done that before, so I'm sure I can do it". Then she raises her arms and tightens her muscles like a weightlifter, as little Longstocking often also did, and repeats, nodding at Klaveness—"she's like Pippi".

Lise Klaveness is facing her, politely saying "yes", "thank you". To be called Pippi is a compliment, you don't find anyone who writes stuff like that for children anymore.

We are at an organic and slightly luxurious restaurant by the sea in Auckland; there's fresh seafood on the menu and inspiration from the Polynesian islands. It's not the first time the ambassador has invited prominent guests to this place. Secretary general Karl-Petter Løken and two NFF board members are here, as well as another secretary general—of the New Zealand Scandinavia Business Association. And a couple of other guests. In other words, Klaveness must make an ever-so-slight adjustment from the doom and gloom at the players' hotel. Now, it's all about business and trading and agreements—but nevertheless, the conversation quickly turns to the match. Klaveness echoes what the girls said as they walked off the pitch—the despair, the rage, the tears, why is everything going wrong for us? She talks about the 8-0 loss against England last year, a match she now calls a trauma, and a trauma that Norway obviously has not shaken off yet. Everyone agrees. It was this match that must have vividly appeared in the minds of the Norwegian players when the first ball went over the defence yesterday.

The way Klaveness describes the England-inflicted trauma is reminiscent of Brazil's loss to Uruguay in the men's World Cup final in 1950. It was a loss the country never could leave behind—a loss that affected national identity and characterised the entire post-war cultural history in Brazil. In fact, the players from 1950 could not rest peacefully in their graves until 2014 when the national team inflicted an even greater shame on the nation, losing 7-1 against Germany in the semi-finals of the second World Cup on home soil. The loss of Norway's women's team against England hasn't had quite the same effect yet, but the influence on the players right now seems to be similar.

It's not all about football at the lunch table. Soon someone's talking about oil and the economy, and then the civil engineer Karl-Petter Løken asks about the presence of Norwegian paint and coating manufacturer Jotun in Auckland, the future of farmed salmon in New Zealand, are whether there are opportunities for exporting lamb to Norway, and shipping—

do the shipping companies from the two countries cooperate well? Then there's discussion about China's takeover of the Pacific Ocean, Maori tattoos, and perhaps how Norwegians can learn a little from how the Maori have integrated into mainstream society. After all, we have our own Indigenous people, the Sami. Then Klaveness says that she watched the game yesterday with FIFA president Gianni Infantino—he looked over her shoulder when she was texting with Karl-Petter Løken during the match: "HELL", "FUCK", "SHIT".

And then Lise had to explain to Gianni what these words, written in Norwegian on her cell phone, meant. A chaplain from the Norwegian church, who is usually stationed in Sydney and present at this lunch, frowns. Løken says apologetically that this is just a way of getting aggression out.

After three hours and two courses, the lunch is over. Klaveness is disappointed because nobody is having dessert. In the taxi back to the hotel, she's on the phone, postponing interview appointments for the next hours. Now there is only one thing on the agenda: being with the team.

For several days, the newspapers in New Zealand write about their team's sensational performance against Norway. The Ferns are the new national heroes, and the team is receiving massive praise. A newspaper cartoonist even makes an analogy to the Moon landing: "A small step for mankind— a giant leap for The Ferns," the text says, accompanied by drawings of Neil Armstrong and Hannah Wilkinson.

The story repeats itself as the championship goes on. The underdogs overachieve. Ireland comes close to beating home favourites Australia. The Philippines' lead against Switzerland is annulled by the VAR, and the Europeans barely manage to land a victory. England must have two attempts at the same penalty to manage a 1–0 victory against Haiti. Vietnam does a great job against the USA, and the reigning champions also get help from the VAR who fails to acknowledge a clear offside, allowing the USA to punctuate the match. And so on. It is one of the big talking points of the World Cup. The smallest nations are no longer to be toyed with. There's no 13–0 (USA-Thailand in the previous World Cup) so far, not even close.

But on this day, Klaveness is in a park just outside central Auckland. There are no footballs nearby. The president has brought her family on this trip. Her wife Ingrid Fosse Sætre is also a former national team player, and they have three children. Today, Klaveness is at a skate park to follow one of her sons. Watching and cheering for their children during leisure activities is one of the joys of parenting. However, with her regular travels, Klaveness must largely leave this joy to her wife.

A pickup truck has two giant speakers onboard this Saturday afternoon in downtown Auckland: skate punk, old American hip-hop, and new Caribbean-inspired New Zealand rap thunders from the car. The park is full of people; the BMX riders have taken over one section, the skaters another. Klaveness finds a place on the outside, watching as her son manoeuvres in the chaos.

"Obviously, it is something I miss. I get to be with them in the evening. I put them to bed every night, I get to hold them close to me. But sometimes I ask myself: how many men would accept what Ingrid accepts now? There must be ways to solve this. Football needs to have women in all positions, including at the top. That means you have to find solutions, financially and in other ways, so that women get the chance to do these jobs. Including during the periods when they have small children," she says.

Two days later, Klaveness goes to Hamilton with the rest of the national team. The rest of the family remains in Auckland, and while Sætre and the two youngest kids stroll around the city, I spend another couple of hours in the skate park with the couple's eldest son.

"Hey, she cheated!"

It is Ada Hegerberg who must take this criticism from her teammates during a warm-up exercise that combines a relay and a version of the three-in-a-row game: each player must sprint ten metres, and then place a vest on a 'playing board' made out of cones on the grass. Then they sprint back and do the exchange. The exercise is perfect for raising the spirits and requires players to be able to think constructively while out of breath and under pressure. Emilie Haavi is struggling to figure out where to put the vest, even though the choice looks easy from outside the heat of the battle. The rest of her team are shouting messages to her—"put it there! NO, NOT THERE ... DOWN LEFT!"

"Hey, take it easy!"

This time it is Tuva Hansen who gets slammed for being too competitive. Klaveness strolls past the girls, and we head to a substitute bench next to the pitch. Once again, rain has replaced sunshine in Auckland's very Norwegian weather, and we find our seats under the roof covering the bench.

"So, you had Gianni Infantino next to you during the first game. Please elaborate!"

"You know about my principle of not reproducing the content of informal conversations."

"Yes. But you must have thought a little about the possibilities you suddenly had? To talk about Qatar, human rights, women's football and things you care about?"

"During the game, it is a bit limited. It was my team that played, too. But we talked about many things. I haven't spoken to him since the day before I gave that speech in Doha."

"Then it was probably natural to just continue from there, from Doha?"

"I wouldn't want to leave without having brought up the things we are concerned about. Not particularly to have a political conversation, but to ensure that he knows where we stand. Which is firstly, the issue of the prize money," she says.

It was a prestigious project for FIFA: the prize money for all players in the World Cup should be increased so that every player gets more than 30,000 US dollars, and the further your team goes in the tournament, the more you get. But just before the World Cup, Infantino stated that "perhaps not all the money would reach the players".

"This is a good move by FIFA, and it is important that they stand by it. That they do not begin to hesitate. For some associations, these will be huge sums. There have probably been requests coming in from federations, someone might have wished that the money could perhaps have been used for many other things. But they can't open that door. He just can't do that. I wanted to say that it is good they made the change, and that it must be carried out even if some eggs are broken along the way."

"Did you understand what he really meant by the statement?"

"I didn't ask what he had said. But I couldn't recognise any of the hesitation that the statement indicates."

"Then it was Qatar, I guess?"

"That whole thing. Qatar, Saudi Arabia coming in with so much money and a will and strategy to invest. Then it is the human rights issue, gender equality and not least LGBQT. After all, football is for everyone. And everyone who wants to invest is able to invest."

"The fact that Saudi Arabia buys Messi as a tourism ambassador and Neymar as a player is a completely natural consequence of the way football has set itself up."

"I was concerned that we have to find a way to talk about the difficult topics. We must have tools and strategies to deal with them."

"But does he at all agree that these things are worth discussing?"

"In my experience, yes. At least in conversations with me. But I can see, and you can see for yourself, that it is something else when he has to deal with 211 associations, and how it goes when he has to comment on such things. But he is an educated man from Europe, he knows that these values exist. As for Qatar, I have a feeling that he is simply relieved that the World Cup is over. That championship was something he inherited, and it was a difficult issue for him."

"It was difficult for quite a few others as well, and they have it even more difficult now."

"All these things he just accepted; we somehow agree on that. And then I said that it would be great if we could meet again and talk about these things."

"Did you ask about the FIFA sub-committee, and the proposal from Norway at the Kigali conference?"

"These things really could build bridges, and the sub-committee for human rights can be a place where we deal with dilemmas. But we don't get a real answer. It is very negative that we do not get an answer. It was important for me to say that."

"Answer to what?"

"We work closely with the Netherlands and Germany on this. UEFA has nominated both me and the secretary general from the Netherlands to the sub- committee. But that committee does not ask UEFA to nominate people. We did it anyway. Then, for a couple of months, I've sent a lot of messages to FIFA, but we haven't received a reply."

"I remember you were so happy in Kigali. But since then, things seem

to have gone slowly?"

"Our proposal in Kigali was enacted, that is satisfactory. But in this world, we have to struggle for every inch, and in the worst-case struggle only to prevent a negative development, towards a point where only mentioning human rights is seen as controversial. I knew the road to implementation would be long. That's where we are now. But we were at a football match, I didn't expect him to sit and ... but he listened, to put it that way."

"There is a lot to deal with in women's football in Europe and America as well. Did you talk about abuse in football?"

"No, actually I didn't. That means we didn't talk about everything I care about."

"Victor Montagliani from Canada is FIFA vice-president and CONCACAF president. He is accused of covering up a sex offender who was also a football coach. The same Montagliani is now present here, he's sending greetings and wishes, basking in the sun as a champion of women's football. Do you think this is okay? What does that do with the confidence that FIFA is trying to rebuild?"

"No, it's not good. Not for the confidence in FIFA, or in him. That's all there is to say about that matter."

"Surely there must be more to say about that matter, in some forum, in a meeting, in one way or another?"

"He has been elected to his position."

"Yes. But when elected politicians break the law or make grave mistakes, they have to go. Elected officials occasionally do things that force them to resign."

"The votes are personal, and he is not someone who will get my vote. People know where we stand. But it would be an illusion to believe that I can change who's getting elected in America, from my position."

"I have no doubt about your opinion, but I wonder if this is even a discussion in the FIFA circles here at the World Cup? Whether such leaders are suitable for FIFA?"

"Leaders who don't take such issues seriously shouldn't be elected at all, obviously. This is something we communicate, directly and indirectly, wherever we are. Unfortunately, I have no power or authority in that issue. What I, we, can ensure, is that Norwegian football should be safe," says

Klaveness, and quickly goes through safe channels for whistleblowers, as well as associated figures and ambitions for Norwegian football on this topic.

"I agree with you, it's as simple as that. We have to pick our battles. The NFF and I are perhaps the most outspoken of all the presidents in the entire world on human rights, and I have been frozen out of some arenas for that reason. For me, it's about getting something done, and now we focus on the issues we have a position on. But gender equality, anti-discrimination and safe sports is what we're indirectly promoting through everything we do."

A Rainy Day in Beautiful Hamilton

With a loss against Switzerland, Norway will be out of the World Cup. It would be a colossal failure based on the ambitions, expectations and preliminary discussions heading into the event. Should New Zealand, as expected, beat the Philippines in a match that begins a couple of hours before ours, it will be difficult to progress even with a draw. Klaveness spends the afternoon at a dinner with sponsors at a steakhouse in Hamilton, a city two hours south of Auckland and an agricultural hotspot that won the prize as New Zealand's most beautiful city in 2020. After dinner, she's heading to the stadium with the players. I call her from outside a football pub near the stadium to ask about her nerves before the game.

"I am an emotional person who works rationally in the emotional sphere," says Klaveness. "Someone must go out of the tournament, that's how it is. What we have to think about is what we gain if we win. We have to focus on the importance of beating Switzerland. They won the bid for the next Euros. They beat us in the men's U-21. I always feel strongly for the national teams when they play. Whether it's the men's, women's, U-21 or the national team of persons of short stature, who play next week. Although, of course, it means a lot when the flagships go out early. The nerves are extra present today," she says.

And while she is talking, I see through the window in the football pub in beautiful Hamilton that the Philippines are 1–0 up against New Zealand. If the result stands, it is more luck than Norway could hope for. But Klaveness keeps her head cool.

"The result is important, but it's more important that our players manage to get out their best. That they dare to try to win and manage to put up a fight. They didn't the last time. The worst thing is to go out with the feeling that they haven't been able to show what they're capable of. That they dare to get mad at their opponent, that Caroline Graham Hansen comes on and shows that she is one of the best players in the world. That is the most important thing today," she says.

Caroline Graham Hansen, the key player at Champions League winner Barcelona, is on the bench. This decision had been debated in the last 24 hours in Norway. Emilie Haavi, playing at Rome in Italy, has taken Graham Hansen's place in the starting line-up, and in the rain at the stadium in Hamilton, the Norwegian girls look fierce on the way out of the tunnel, during the warm-up, during the national anthem and in the final pep talk on the turf.

Then Ada Hegerberg walks out of the ring and resolutely continues towards the dressing room. What's happening? Sophie Román Haug (Liverpool) takes off her coat, while the other 10 players have found their positions on the pitch. Hegerberg does not come out again, and Román Haug is jogging towards the mid-circle. Our most important game in many years kicks-off and neither of Norway's two world-class attacking superstars are on the pitch. Nobody understands anything, not even the players out on the field. In the press box, everyone is confused, and we're all looking at the newspaper journalist from *VG*, famous for knowing all the gossip about the superstars. Now she must write something about what's going on."

"She felt something in the groin," writes Klaveness in a text message about Hegerberg's injury.

That exact wording comes as an official statement from the NFF's press team shortly afterwards, and the stadium announcer informs the crowd of the change shortly after kick-off—fans didn't even notice what had happened and thought Hegerberg played the first few minutes of the match.

Norway is a different team today. They dare to try. They look for chances. Román Haug has a dangerous header. The ball flows easily between the players. In defence, they fight. Caroline Graham Hansen comes on after 56 minutes. She quickly influences the game with classic dribbles from the edge of the pitch towards the box. She fires a couple of dangerous shots.

But Switzerland's goalkeeper has a good game and is named the player of the match. It ends 0-0. Nevertheless, apparently there are no disgruntled girls who go through the mixed zone afterwards.

"I think there were girls hungry for revenge who went out there today," says attacker Frida Maanum (Arsenal).

"In a way, we are satisfied with the performance, but we would have liked to have some goals," says captain and defender Maren Mjelde.

"Why is it such an incredibly different team that we see today?"

"I would like to know that myself," says midfielder Guro Reiten.

"After an experience like the last one. The worst thing as a player, when the match is over, is ... when you have the feeling, I wasn't myself today. Today, no matter what happened, we were going to walk off the pitch and say we did everything we could. I feel we can say that. This is something that can represent us as a team," she says.

But not everyone is as satisfied. At the same time as Reiten says that the performance represents them as a team, Caroline Graham Hansen drops a bomb in a TV interview with Viaplay/TV2, just a few metres away.

"I feel I have been stepped on for a whole year. Everyone says all the time that we have to stand together as a nation and a team, I feel like I've been on the receiving end," she says, adding that she feels like her hands are tied, and through a reference to a novel by the Danish-Norwegian author Aksel Sandemose, says there is no room for individuality in the Norwegian squad.

Graham Hansen did not play international football from August 2022 to April 2023. Now, it's like she's blowing on smouldering embers. Immediately, everyone in Norway is talking about the internal affairs of the national squad. What is Caroline Graham Hansen unhappy about? Is she in a row with the coach? Is it only bitterness because she started on the bench? Or anything else? An argument with Ada Hegerberg? Dissatisfaction with the tactics, the morale, the build-up, her teammates?

Back home, commentators are writing and talking at high speed, and while the Norwegian player bus silently rolls through the night from Hamilton to Auckland, several suggest that Graham Hansen should be sent home for making her statements. *Aftonbladet*, a newspaper from our neighbour country Sweden, calls Norway "the World Cup's biggest drama queens"—not without a decent amount of satisfaction between the lines. The future of both Graham Hansen and the Norwegian national team seems very uncertain.

The next morning in Auckland, the announced press conference is postponed by an hour, allegedly due to the late return last night. When it starts, Graham Hansen enters the podium. "I just want to apologise for my statements after the game. I'm just a human being with a lot of feelings. It's been a tough few days (...) Yesterday, the emotions got the better of me." It appears that the same apology was given to the players earlier in the morning. After Graham Hansen's statements, coach Hege Riise and players Guro Reiten and Vilde Bøe Risa enter the podium one after the other, and they all say that the apology has been accepted.

Case closed–Caroline Graham Hansen is ready for the Philippines after a 12-hour roller coaster ride.

Klaveness and Graham Hansen played together in Stabæk over a decade ago when Klaveness was 31 and Graham Hansen 14. They have known each other for a long time and have had many long conversations about football and other things in life, both during the last year and earlier. This evening, they had another.

"The first thing I said was that she had made a good game coming on from the bench. Then I said that if she regrets something that was said in the mixed zone, it is usually possible to sort things out. You can say sorry."

"How was the atmosphere on the bus home? An hour-and-a-half through the dark, after a post-match situation like that?"

"It wasn't really a big topic. We were relieved to be alive in the tournament, with the possibility of qualifying for the next stage. I sat at the front and talked to Hege and the team. We obviously wondered how we were going to make things work out," she says.

At the back of the bus, the girls sat with phones in hand and chatted, with or without mobile data left for surfing. Well past midnight, they returned to Auckland. Early the next morning, Klaveness held a quick board meeting on Teams (which was planned) where half the participants were at home in Norway. It was decided that the football president should take a few steps outside of her usual work zone to help calm things down.

"I come from the law, I have been a court mediator, so now I was on home ground. Caroline was sorry for the attention the comments had drawn to the rest of the team, she wanted to apologise. Remember that she is one of the world's best players. Swiss and German newspapers speculated on how they could manage to stop her, the *New York Times* has written about how big a threat she is. Then she is benched. It is difficult for everyone to be benched, but this gives the benching an extra dimension. In addition, she has been upset for a year because she was taken out of the group of captains right after Hege took over. Then comes the adrenaline from the match, and all the questions from the press. She shouldn't have reacted the way she did, but these were the reasons," says Klaveness.

"There must have been someone who has caught that she has been upset for a whole year after being taken out of the group of captains?"

"Of course, she and Hege have had conversations about this, guaranteed. I'm not in [on] the details between coach and player," says Klaveness.

"How is it possible that this comes out after a super-important game in the World Cup? I thought this was the kind of thing you're supposed to dig up in routine conversations between coach and player?"

"This is in the relationship between player and coach. I don't know about that, and it's not something I should enter as football president," she says. "My role was simply to help both player and coach as much as I can.

Three days later, the Philippines are waiting on the other half of the pitch. Graham Hansen is back in the forward line, and after six minutes Norway takes the lead. Graham Hansen scores herself after half an hour. The final score is 6-0, Norway finally plays well, and the team narrowly manages to go on from the group stage. In the round of 16, Japan awaits. They have emerged as outsiders for the title after a strong 4-0 win over Spain.

For the rest of the World Cup, underdogs doing well remains a major narrative: Jamaica knocks out Brazil, Morocco knocks out Germany, South Africa knocks out Italy and Argentina. Colombia advances to the quarter-finals. Nigeria is beaten in a penalty shootout against England after pressing the European Championship champions for the entire match. The Africans but can go home with their heads held high. Norway, on the other hand, plays very poorly in the round of 16. The tactics seems to be only defensive, simply to keep everyone behind the ball and try to allow Japan as little room as possible. And maybe, *maybe,* a counterattack could be created at some point.

It doesn't work forwards or backwards, and Norway loses 3–1 against Japan.

Lise Klaveness has one thing in common with all of the former leaders at Ullevaal—Terje Svendsen, Pål Bjerketvedt, Martin Sjögren and many others. They have used the same explanatory model for why Norway has dropped like a stone in FIFA rankings, and in less than 20 years gone from being a world leader to mediocrity in women's football. The reason, according to all the men mentioned above, and Klaveness in several interviews, is that all the major football nations have begun to invest in women's football. Spain, England, Italy and so on. It is impossible for tiny Norway to keep up, even though we had a big lead that lasted until the years after the Olympic gold in Sydney, 2000.

"But the games of Nigeria, Colombia, Morocco, South Africa, Jamaica and several others in this World Cup show that the narrative from Ullevaal is false. Many small nations are better than the heavyweights. Has the federation unwillingly convinced the Norwegian players that they no longer have a chance, because 'big nations' have started investing in women's football?"

"Yes, I think so. We have become both too offensive and too defensive. When we won the World Cup in 1995 and the Olympics in 2000, it was because someone seized the opportunity. We have worked our way backwards from there. At the same time, the market outside has completely changed. In the 1990s, our own economy was similar to the English. Now England is astronomically much bigger. But that must not prevent us from seizing the role of the challenger! You are right, for many years we have been too defensive, and spent many years thinking about everything we cannot do. This must not hold us back. And then it must be said that Nigeria was knocked out in the same round as us.

"Yes. But many smaller teams performed fantastically, with an attitude we haven't seen in Norway for many years. Like Jamaica."

"Absolutely, the development is incredible, with so many teams making their mark for the first time and giving fantastic performances. We need the mentality that tells us we can go all the way, that makes us fearless challengers. You must be precise enough to make the girls believe it. Instead, we have worked our way backwards since the 1990s. Whereas Jamaica works from below and when they win, the whole nation is with them," says Klaveness.

✷ ✷ ✷

Although the time in New Zealand is primarily used to focus on the matches, Klaveness also squeezes in some football politics. Meetings with 'our allies': i.e., the Netherlands, Switzerland and Germany.

"And then I had a meeting with Gianni's second-in-command. Fatma."

"Haha. Lise and Fatma! That was a surprise."

"Hehe, sure. After all, she will step down as FIFA secretary general now. She knows a lot about how to make Muslim girls begin [playing] football. So, we can collaborate on that. She is from Senegal; she knows how to reach out. You have to go into the villages, talk to the mothers."

"But Fatma has not exactly distinguished herself as a strong campaigner for increasing the participation of young Muslim girls through her years as secretary general? She is considered to be one of the least active and independent secretary generals in FIFA's history?"

"I have had my fights with Fatma. But she has a lot of knowledge about exactly this, and then, as I see it, there is no reason not to try to use this knowledge for something."

The Kiss

Of the underdogs, Colombia went the farthest. They went out in the quarter-finals against England in a match that could've gone either way. The other three semi-finalists were Spain, Sweden and the home team Australia, with superstar Sam Kerr half injured but back in the starting line-up. While these matches were being played, Klaveness travelled home to Norway with her family before travelling back to Oceania again to witness the final. It was Spain who won in the end, after having controlled England in the final 90 minutes of the tournament. Then everything exploded.

"I was there in the stands," says Klaveness.

"I was sitting with Vanda [Sigurdgeirsdottir], Iceland's football president, and I was jet-lagged and disoriented. I had stopped sleeping, and on the day of the final I could only drink water, I didn't have the strength to do anything. During the final I just sat quietly and watched. When the ceremony started, I saw both Luis [Rubiales] and Debbie [Hewitt] giving the players a big hug. My first reaction was that this is really nice! Here we have presidents who care about the players. Then he starts lifting them. I'm informal myself, and I'm thinking, okay, fine by me, but will there be reactions? Then I actually said to Vanda: now he has to lift Jorge Vilda too, Spain's coach. He didn't, and I said, 'too bad'. All in all, he seemed a bit too eager. And then we just left," says Klaveness.

Shortly afterwards, the television images from the ceremony in Sydney were zoomed, paused and shared. They showed Rubiales grabbing the head of Spain captain Jennifer Hermoso and planting a firm kiss on her lips.

"I see the pictures right after the match, at the same time as everyone else. It is completely unacceptable," says Klaveness, and in the good spirit of a lawyer, she mentions the mitigating circumstances. He is an individual, he is genuinely happy, and with all the conflicts in Spanish women's football in the back of his mind—now they could all finally be together as champions of the world.

"Then five minutes pass, and he makes everything worse. Hermoso comes from Barcelona, the club of the players who protested against the federation. She can't let something like that pass. It is a politically dangerous act towards her, although he would not commit a sexual assault with all the world's television cameras on him."

"But the fact that he did it shows that he thinks it's okay, and that says quite a lot about what the culture is like?"

"Exactly. That was my point," says Klaveness.

In the weeks after the World Cup, the storm blows around Rubiales. Football players all over the world declare their support for Hermoso, including Norwegians Ada Hegerberg and Caroline Graham Hansen. A few male players do the same, such as Hector Bellerin from Spain, who is always politically engaged.

Writers and commentators from different countries declare that Rubiales must resign. He makes a speech of defence in front of the rest of the Spanish Football Federation (RFEF), and it culminates in him shouting:

"I'm not going to resign! I'm not going to resign!" The speech is greeted with a standing ovation, and in the cheering RFEF crowd are both the Spanish women's national team coach Jorge Vilda and men's national team coach Luis de la Fuente. The message is clear: the federation backs Rubiales, not Hermoso.

But the criticism does not stop. Andrés Iniesta, who scored the winning goal when the men won the World Cup in 2010, enters the stage. He also believes Rubiales must go. Xavi Hernández, who together with Iniesta formed what many believe is one of the best midfield pairs in history, says the same. Then, in a bizarre twist, Rubiales's mother goes on a hunger strike in a church in the south of Spain. She calls the criticism of her son an "inhumane, bloodthirsty hunt". Thus, Rubiales has both his family and the association behind him. But not many others, and after a few days his mother gives up her hunger strike. She has to go to hospital for an examination but is discharged after a few hours.

"When he doesn't back down, and instead talks about taking legal action against the player, he fuels a dangerous anti-feminism, and it turns into an alt-right thing. Then he loses me. Dangerous ideas are stirred up," says Klaveness at the end of August, back in Norway after the days of commuting between Oceania and Scandinavia.

"You had meetings with him this spring. Then you said that he was 'very nice', 'a president you get energy from'. It was a very positive meeting, you said at the time. Do you feel cheated now?"

"I found him to be an attentive and energetic person who did not engage in positioning. Because of the big conflict they have had, he got to know the team. He talked to the players, and that never happens. Often the presidents don't even know the names of the players. He was about the only president I spoke to who was somewhat concerned with the women's team. He supported me, he voted for us, my experience was that he was genuinely concerned about getting people from the sport and the pitches into political positions. Many others did the opposite. He deserves that I say this."

"Nevertheless?"

"He must resign now. He has behaved unacceptably. Nobody talks about the World Cup anymore, only about Rubiales. It can't be like that. Now he has to protect the sport. He is in a bubble where he is fighting for his life. But it becomes impossible when the pictures are there, it becomes a symbol for the entire history of women's football. You are there when there are good days, but as soon as it is over, discrimination against women is a big problem. The World Cup champions have withdrawn from the national team because of this. He must go. I have contacted him and his assistants and expressed this. Not that I think it has any influence, but still," she says.

"This is UEFA's vice-president. We already talked about FIFA's vice-president and the head of Canada's World Cup 2026 who covered up a sex offender so that he could continue to train young girls. Shouldn't they get the same message from you?"

"Yes, but Rubiales is a colleague in UEFA, a person I know a little and met with on several occasions. So, my position was a little better here than in the one you mention at FIFA," she says.

During this period, one event follows another. First, Rubiales is suspended by FIFA. Gradually, more and more Spanish politicians begin to demand his resignation. But sport is "autonomous". It must be run by its own organisations and legal systems without interference from politicians. The RFEF therefore contacts UEFA, and requests that all Spanish clubs be suspended from their tournaments. The argument is that Spain breaks the rules on the autonomy of sport because of their politicians' interference. This is seen as a desperate move to save Rubiales—it means that both Real Madrid and Barcelona will not be allowed to participate in the Champions League this year. This, the RFEF thinks, will create so much dissatisfaction that people will "switch sides" and support Rubiales.

But that's not how it works out. RFEF's request is rejected. Jorge Vilda, the applauding and disliked women's coach, is stepping down. Then Rubiales finally has had enough. He gives up and resigns as RFEF president. And his seat on the UEFA board that Klaveness tried to be elected to? It will remain empty until the next election.

4
AUTUMN

In these busy August days, everyone involved in football in Norway is waiting for something else: the evaluation of the World Cup in Oceania. Many strong adjectives are used in the preliminary reviews and comments. The evaluation is going to be tough, rock-hard, brutally honest, direct, raw and intense, with no mercy. One thing is the disappointing results. Another thing is the even more disappointing performances on the pitch. The big question is Hege Riise. Does the coach have a future as the leader of the national team? As the incident with Graham Hansen showed, she has failed to maintain harmony in the squad. But her contract expires in 2025. Is it even possible for her to continue after such a disappointing World Cup? The NFF's presentation of their World Cup evaluation is postponed again and again and again. Klaveness is tight-lipped in all statements. Even on Instagram, she's quiet.

Then, on September 1, the news arrives: Riise resigns. Thus, the NFF came to the opposite conclusion with Riise than they did with men's coach Ståle Solbakken, who also had very bad results this year.

"Everyone likes and respects Hege. I have played with her, there has never been a bad word between us. She has crazy credentials. It was her turn to take over the team," says Klaveness.

In the same way as it was "Ståle's turn" when Mr. Solbakken got the job as men's coach several years after he was offered the job for the first time but declined because of a more tempting offer from Bundesliga club, Köln.

"But we knew that Hege's style was different from many," she continues.

This style is more reserved, with few big words and gestures. According to various media, the assistant coaches often held tactical meetings with the players. During the World Cup, national broadcaster NRK wrote—based on "sources in the squad"—that there was dissatisfaction with Riise's half-time talk during the match against New Zealand. Anyway, with all the turmoil and poor performances this summer, the board was now unanimous.

"It is absolutely not about giving someone the blame. We had to make a choice, and the focus had to be [on] what we believe will work out for the near future. Thinking about what we've been through, we considered that a change at this point is inevitable. I am very happy that she wants to join and continue to work in the new position in the NFF," says Klaveness. The ex-coach will continue in the federation, with severance pay until December 2024, in a newly created position as "chief adviser for women's football". In other words, Norway gets yet another relocated former football coach with a high salary in an office in the hallways at Ullevaal.

"It is an important position, she has credibility, and the coaches will be confident with her... It feels good," says Klaveness.

Another important point when Klaveness talks about the evaluation after the World Cup is comparisons. Which nations should we compare ourselves to, and how? We seemed to have no chance against Japan. At the same time, the number of grassroot players in Norway is significantly higher than in Japan.

"But that is not necessarily relevant for the top," says Klaveness. "England is academy-governed. Japan operates from top to bottom in a pyramid designed with top player development as the main focus. In Norway, we have more of an all-for-one spirit, we're a very strong grassroot nation. We want as many players as possible because we are a real people's movement. We will never test six-year-olds to see if they have the potential to become top players."

But what do we do to ensure that our model is still competitive even at the top? According to Klaveness, the answers are the same on the men's and women's sides. It is about strengthening cooperation between top clubs, between national and county federations, sharing information, having better youth coaches and a wider youth pyramid.

"We don't want the top clubs to vacuum-clean the markets, but we don't want the opposite either, that people are being held back. You need to strengthen the coordinating procedures. If you leave it to the coaches, everyone will only think about their own team. Find out which clubs and environments are leading the others and reinforce these. Who will ensure that our model, as a people's movement, still is intact, at the same time as we beat Japan in the World Cup?" asks Klaveness, and it's clear that she doesn't think the answers are easy either.

More Rainy Football

And with that, autumn has arrived for Lise Klaveness. The games in Norway have been played for a few weeks already after a month's break in July during the World Cup. The president continues with the activities from this spring: super volunteers, club visits, international matches, street teams and seminars. Sarpsborg, Drammen, Barcelona, Ullevaal, Lillehammer, Morocco.

On September 14, in the Aksla clubhouse outside Ålesund on the windy Norwegian west coast, Klaveness once again talks about her good friend from childhood—the ball. And about the football juggling on the way to and from school. In front of her, 23 men and seven women sit in a circle. Klaveness talks about the top versus the grassroots.

"Ada and Erling came from small clubs, not professional academy clubs. So, we can have confidence in our system," she says, and then rubber granules become a topic. Afterwards, it's selfie time in the wind.

When you enter Color Line Stadion, the home ground of Aalesunds FK, the football club in the city that Klaveness visits, you are met with a massive smell of meatballs.

"I don't eat meat," says Klaveness before the lunch is to be consumed.

The program at Color Line is a fixed one that's similar to her other club visits. She holds an inspirational talk with the women's team on the pitch, and then delivers a PowerPoint lecture for other club workers afterwards, indoors. She tells a story about when she dropped her iPhone on the subway line the day before, already documented on Instagram, and the audience gets hooked on her other stories. Juggling the ball in her childhood is brought up for the second time in 24 hours. Next, the climate crisis and other social themes are linked to football. Her Aalesund FK presentation that follows goes the same way and also highlights the club's investment in dementia prevention for children. It is a well-known fact that footballers are more susceptible to dementia than many others, which has contributed to the banning of heading exercises in children's football in many countries.

"When you hear Infantino and the others talk about women's football, they always talk about daughters. Always! They know little about women's football. But they have daughters," says Klaveness from the stage.

Quite right. On the Twitter account of Victor Montagliani, the FIFA vice-president and CONCACAF president who failed to inform players about their coach being guilty of sexual abuse, the football politician has highlighted that he is a "proud girl dad".

That evening, as Klaveness drives to the clubhouse of Blindheim, another club on the edge of the city of Ålesund, not far from where the ferry goes over the fjord and into the countryside, a small boy in a Spider-Man costume stands urinating next to the football pitch, as many other boys do next to other pitches around the country.

"My aim is to visit all the county federations. After all, this is our country, if you don't go out and meet all the people, you don't understand anything. I get energy from this; if you're out on a trip, you might as well move around as much as possible, you can't just go back to the hotel for the evening. You must believe that what you do matters," she says.

There's another round of greetings, selfies, tricks and stories about her childhood football juggling and recent meetings with Infantino. The whole evening is spent at the Blindheim clubhouse, and the next day, Klaveness takes the ferry to Ulsteinvik. The town where the TV series *Heimebane* took place, about the female coach who took over a men's team in top football, with star actor Ane Dahl Torp in the lead role. A couple of years later, the same thing happened in real life when Renate Blindheim became coach for semi-professional club Sotra in the third tier. It was a TV series that even the most male-chauvinist football fans dug. In real life, Ulsteinvik is the hometown of the Hødd club.

"We are part of a systematic discriminatory culture. Soccer is the world's biggest sport for girls. Both abroad and in Norway. On the UEFA board, there are only men. The fact that they are men is not the problem. The problem is that there are only men who have no expertise in women's football on the board. This is important for Hødd as well," she says in today's lecture.

The last lunch of the trip is taken at Høddvoll Stadium, and as Klaveness enters the canteen and looks over the selection of hot food, she states that "it is easier to be a woman than a vegetarian in Norwegian football!"

Another Surprise

Just a few days after Klaveness returned from Ulsteinvik, the news came that UEFA had reversed a position of principle taken a couple of years ago: Russia should be allowed to participate in next year's U-17 European Championship. Qualification for the event was to start the next week. Suddenly, everyone was in a hurry. It was urgent to get things organised before the qualifiers. But both the media and football leaders were on fire, and the debate was fierce.

"It came as a surprise to everyone," says Klaveness in the middle of October.

The decision was taken at a board meeting at a hotel in Cyprus on September 26, after a proposal put forward by UEFA president Aleksander Čeferin towards the end of the meeting. One of his arguments was that it was not right to "punish children" by excluding them from championships. Several ExCo football presidents spoke up against the president. The external observers did the same at the UEFA meeting, which very rarely happens.

"It was probably an unusually lively discussion for a UEFA board meeting," says Klaveness.

"Was there any pressure on UEFA from somewhere to lift the sanctions against Russia?"

"I really don't know. We were all caught off guard. And it's not just an impression I have, because I've spoken to many people who sit on the UEFA board who were present at the meeting. The suggestion set minds ablaze. But Dyukov is on the board," says Klaveness.

Alexander Dyukov is the Russian football president, chairman of Gazprom and former president of the Gazprom-owned club that Vladimir Putin cheers for, Zenit St. Petersburg.

"The timing probably had something to do with the IOC [International Olympic Committee] wanting to include Russian athletes in the Olympics," she says.

IOC president Thomas Bach, like FIFA president Infantino, has cultivated a close relationship with Putin for many years.

"In addition, the UEFA leaders are probably taking a lot of pressure about including the senior football team. U-15s are already included; they are in the children's category and not covered by the boycott. It was only U-17 they could add," says Klaveness.

Danish president Jesper Møller voted for Čeferin's proposal. So did Swedish sports president Karl-Erik Nilsson, who was also football president until Fredrik Reinfeldt took over last year, and he is still UEFA's vice-president. The proposal was accepted by the board. Russia was back, and it was a huge victory for Putin and Dyukov. Klaveness quickly gathered the board of the NFF for a meeting, and afterwards said to the press that Norway would not play against Russia in the U-17 qualifiers that were scheduled to start the following week. Poland, Romania, England and Sweden did the same. A little later, Denmark followed. In other words, at the UEFA meeting in Cyprus, Møller and Nilsson voted the opposite of what their own federations and countries stood for. For the next few days, Klaveness's team worked in high gear.

"Then it was about doing research, using all contacts. To confirm what opinions people had. I was messaging with people, [and] Christian and Magnus tried to find documents," she says about two of her colleagues— her advisor and the chief of staff at Ullevaal.

"I quickly understood that there is real opposition, [and] that it is possible to have the decision reversed. It was [only] a very short time until the qualification was about to begin," she says.

But after a week of pressure and massive media attention which led, among other things, to Karl-Erik Nilsson resigning as sports president in

Sweden, the UEFA decision was reversed. Russia would not be welcomed back after all.

"It is an example that internal democracy is alive. It's heavy, but there are possibilities. It is completely crazy that such a suggestion could go through in the first instance. That the Swedish or Danish presidents, for example, did not pull the emergency brake," she says.

"You have talked a lot about FIFA and UEFA having to rebuild confidence. What happens to the people's confidence in the federations when the Danish and Swedish presidents act contrary to the views of their own FAs [football associations]?"

"I'm not going to talk about them. But this is the general problem, the whole structure is such that your choices are based on relations. In a way, you are not representing your federation. There is little internal debate before anyone is elected, nor is there any regional debate about who should stand for election. When we ran for the UEFA board, it became clear that we were kind of challenging Sweden and Denmark, since they in a way represent the Nordic region in UEFA. And I didn't know that. But then it's important that the rest of the Nordic countries like us are included before any decisions are made," says Klaveness.

As this case showed, the Danish and Swedish UEFA board members neither represented their own nor the rest of the Nordic countries.

"It was such a clear argument in Lisbon that we are together in regions. Then I actually expect to be involved. I expect that those who represent us regionally in the Nordics involve us systematically. Before and after ExCo meetings. But that didn't happen here," says Klaveness.

In the case of Russia, the children were used as an argument. At the same time as Klaveness and the NFF worked behind the scenes to make UEFA turn around, the situation of some other children ended up in the world's spotlight: the children of Israel and Palestine.

"Spanish defender Hector Bellerin once stated that the sanctions against Russia were hypocritical, as they were not repeated against, for example, Saudi Arabia because of the war against Yemen, or against Israel because of the Palestine situation. Should the football world come up with sanctions against Israel? They are going to host a European Championship soon, but will that be possible?

"First, I must say that what is happening in the Middle East now is absolutely terrible," she says, a few days after Israel started dropping bombs on Gaza.

The Israeli government says the bombing is a response, a kind of self-defence, after the terrorist attack from the Palestinian group Hamas on October 7 that killed around 1,200 Israelis, most of them civilians.

"My starting point otherwise is very clear, and that is that everyone must be allowed to play football, regardless of what their state does. We will play against Palestine, Israel, Russia, USA, Iran. It is a philosophical position. But the issue here was that Dyukov, who is a Gazprom director, also sits on the UEFA board, and Putin has constantly used football as propaganda, and it is a European joint action that also extends beyond sports. But ... you're saying that Israel will host the European Championships?"

"A youth Euros, a few years in the future. Israeli prime minister Netanyahu has already used it as propaganda with photos of himself and Čeferin after the award [of hosting rights]."

"It is not certain that football can be played there, and the situation being like it is at this point, it's impossible," she says about a month after the terror attacks, a month that has been filled with endless bombing of the Gaza Strip, resulting in 10,000 deaths, most of them civilians and many of them children.

"Awarding championships is something completely different than playing against countries. Because then it is about a lot of other things. Showcasing, security ..." says Klaveness.

The championship is scheduled to take place in 2027, but in 2023 it does not look like safety could be guaranteed to anyone playing there.

"It's not like the NFF sits and discusses whether a two-state solution is best in the Israel/Palestine case. At the same time, the actual war *is* something we talk about. Because this is a terrible thing, and we are a people's movement, so we cannot be passive when all this happens. There are a lot of people in Norway who really want us to show solidarity. The best thing we can do now is not to boycott any country, but to use our platforms to provide humanitarian aid. In other words, we make it easy for people to get involved, by, for example, tipping money into organisations," she says.

A couple of days later, the NFF president posts a picture of herself at a demonstration in front of the Norwegian parliament where she encourages financial support for both the Red Cross and Save the Children organisations. The text accompanying the photo reads: "Children and civilians should NEVER be targets in an armed conflict."

Fear of Empty Stadiums

It is the day before Norway meets France in the Nations League for Olympic qualification. 2023 was to be the year when Caroline Graham Hansen and Ada Hegerberg finally got to shine together, when we were to fight back during the World Cup in New Zealand. Instead, we are second last in the Nations League group, with a draw against Austria the best result so far. A win against France will feel much like when the mediocre Norwegian men sensationally beat world-class England in 1981.

"We face a better team, we'll just have to see how it goes," says Klaveness soberly from her office on the fourth floor at Ullevaal.

She has just returned from another club visit, Harstad IL this time.

"They have a fantastic program, with organised football for people with special disabilities. There are a lot of people training, they have really got the thing running," she says.

In the Hålogaland county federation in the north of Norway, only Mjølner and Harstad cater for people with disabilities playing football.

"Why does such a thing work perfectly well in some clubs, while [in] others it doesn't work at all?"

"The answer is always that one person or another has taken responsibility and started to pull strings. And then it turns out that the project is able to stay alive. The reason at Harstad is Hugo Kjelseth, who has been a super volunteer for many years.

"There's no doubt you are genuinely excited and very engaged in this. But you say it has everything to do with a super volunteer who has taken a huge load of unpaid work to make it happen. What do you personally think about this, and the distance to the other side of football where you can find the extreme salaries of Manchester City's Erling Braut Haaland and the other stars, and the bubbles they live in?

"I've had those discussions with quite a few people who say it is unfair, which of course it is. But the answer is always that he still earns much less than many people in the world of finance. After all, he plays in a sport that is the biggest and most competitive in the world. And those businessmen, like billionaire Kjell Inge Røkke, don't deserve it anymore."

"But football is our area, our world, so we do have to talk about what it's like in football?"

"Yes, yes, but if you want my answer, you will get it. And my answer is that those forces work in football. If you could redistribute and make things exactly even in all industries, that would be fantastic. But it doesn't work that way in society. Not in Norway, even though we have social democracy. He does not have a salary that comes from Norwegian budgets, he earns the same for the national team as Caroline Graham Hansen and the women do. We have a football model that is more egalitarian than [the one] out in the world, so my view on this is complex. But we are part of a bigger logic. I don't think financial profit should be seen as an enemy. We need profit to finance what we're doing with football for people with special needs."

"But isn't it Erling's profit that gives money to Harstad Tigers? And his finances come from—"

"Now you have *your* political views, wait, and you will get *my* answer. My point is that we are in complete agreement, it's just that you don't have the same responsibility as I do. Erling's money is England, it's not money I have. What we need is for him to be such a big star that we get full stadiums, so Ullevaal will be filled with children. We are one of the very few federations that also runs grassroots football, but at the same time we follow what's going on internationally. That means I can't go too far in saying that it's terrible. But I still think that there are absurd differences when it comes to money, that is my view. Just as I wish that your magazine *Josimar* had written just as much about women's and men's football, but that is not the case."

"As far as the economy is concerned, has football itself facilitated the current situation through the way it has operated in recent decades?"

"Yes, and then there is enormous inflation, which is absurd. But at some point, the bubble can burst, quite simply. It is okay that money comes from Saudi Arabia, but we also have this fear-of-empty-stadiums issue. We include that in our presentations. At some point, you [could] lose the essence so much that you actually risk losing football's popularity. It could happen, you never know.

VAR

The possibility of simply stopping to go to the stadium to watch football is the background scenario in another debate which was close to boiling point in the week before the France game. The Norwegian supporters campaigned heavily against the VAR via demonstrations in the stands and in debates on both social media and traditional media outlets all over the country. They also became members of their respective clubs to make them vote against the VAR in the next Norwegian football assembly. It was a joint movement, and on the other side of the table was the NFF and Lise Klaveness who introduced the VAR in Norway before the 2023 season.

"Isn't it inspiring to see how Norwegian supporters get involved in football democracy and join their clubs in an attempt to get the VAR removed from Norwegian arenas?"

"Yes, we really are lucky in Norway to have supporters working through the democratic structures. The challenge with the engagement with the VAR is that it's about something that has already been adopted. I am the chairman of a company that has made a decision on a project which must now be implemented," says Klaveness.

There are well-known arguments that are put forward in the debate. Long waiting times before decisions, continued disagreement after VAR interventions, and not least that the immediacy disappears from the games along with some of the most important feelings in football. The situation mirrors the one in 2022 when the debate about the Norwegian boycott of Qatar raged. Then, as now, the Norwegian supporters become members of their clubs. Their aim is to launch proposals and win votes against the VAR, so that the clubs in turn can force the NFF to overturn its decision through the football parliament.

"Personally, I really have no prestige in this matter. I was not [the] board leader when the decision was made. But the VAR project is important for us in Norwegian football. Many people have been involved. They have spent time and resources. Not least, it's important for the referees. It is important that, on the one hand, we do not wear blinders and only defend decisions because they have been made. Of course, we have to listen to critique. At the same time, we must ensure that the top clubs who were in favour of VAR must have a very good look at what the consequences are if they are now going to oppose it," she says.

"It's about our values, it's about being in the terraces, the immediacy, it's very easy for me to get used to it. Nobody likes breaks of five, six or seven minutes. Whether it's because of pyro[technics] or VAR. I don't think it's any cooler to wait for the match because of a lot of smoke," she says, with reference to the growing interest in pyro among Norwegian supporters in recent years.

In the VAR debate, the top Norwegian clubs have been represented by Cato Haug, leader of the NTF (Norsk Toppfotball), which is the name of the organisation of the clubs. Among the things that Haug said to the newspaper *VG* was this: "If it is professionally stupid to scrap VAR, then someone must come up with a professional view." This, and several other statements where 'professionalism' has been used as an argument for the VAR, has caused supporters to accuse football management of newspeak and arrogance.

"It is unclear what 'professional' actually means in these arguments?"

"It was Cato who said that, not me. For my part, it's not only about what's a professional view on VAR. It is about my job as chairman, and a decision that has been made. If there is to be a rematch on this, then the clubs must know about the consequences and the timing for when a change is an opportunity, and we're only one year into a project that is scheduled for many years. It is about understanding this, and at the same time understanding that football also is emotional. The emotional experience of a football game is affected if you're taking away the immediacy. This is no doubt a relevant argument. Another relevant argument is that we're doing everything we can to get fair decisions and a league table that is as correct as possible. But we're going to work really hard to improve VAR. That's our focus."

"In the strategy plan of [the] NTF and [the] NFF, it is stated that 'the project shall contribute to investigate possibilities for commercial opportunities in VAR'. What do [the] NFF and [the] NTF mean?

"I don't know. In the strategic plan of the federation, this is not specified, only that we had an aim of introducing VAR. Not primarily because it creates a lot of good television entertainment. At least as far as I know. Many supporters don't want to discuss solutions, they only want VAR to be gone.

That's totally fair. In any case, I will present solutions. Because my job is to present solutions and because the solutions exist. While some people just want it away anyway," says Klaveness.

She suggests that it might be possible to find some kind of "common ground". For example, if the VAR decisions were made with less delay? Or that only the biggest mistakes were caught by VAR? Would the fans still be just as categorically against it?

"VAR is a scalable project," she says.

But many football people disagree. From the supporters' side, the NFF and NTF's arguments have not been convincing. On Twitter (X), people have reacted to several statements, such as this one from Klaveness: "If the debate and decisions are to take place in an action form where a pure black/white logic applies, we are in danger of underestimating important considerations."

Cato Haug also said: "There was something similar with the Qatar debate. Such actions are never ideal. I was hoping that you wouldn't get actions like that, where you mobilise on single issues. But that you would rather help develop football continuously."

Haug was referring to the Qatar debate which led up to Klaveness's speech in Doha, the speech that has given her a platform worldwide, as a burden for Norwegian football.

"Are there voices in Ullevaal that simply do not like the Norwegian football democracy?"

"If so, it is something we have to address. We should actually say that we welcome democracy. I don't think I would say that there are systematic forces with such opinions. But I think, for example, that many professional groups may feel a bit overrun if there are only headlines from one side. And I absolutely do believe that there are voices in Norway who are simply used to believing that everything happens through the county federations and the traditional structures of football. Then, when a small group of people who are supporters take over, with negation, it simply creates a fear. It's more about that than about shady powers working in secret. I thought the Qatar case was fantastic because it became a real debate throughout our structures," she says.

And finally, about VAR: "There is no one who wants to lose face. I am working very hard to ensure *this* isn't what's defining our moves in this matter. It's just a project we've introduced. [It's] A very important project involving many and is important to many. But we'll always be available to supporters and members for discussion."

World Cup 2034

The year is coming to an end, and Bayern München announces that they have a new sponsor. This summer, the German club ended its collaboration with Qatar Airways. Visit Rwanda is now presented as a new major partner.

Around the same time in November, Gianni Infantino publishes the following Instagram post: "The next two editions of the FIFA World Cup will be held in Africa (Morocco), Europe (Portugal and Spain)—with three matches played in South America (Argentina, Paraguay, and Uruguay)—in 2030, and in Asia (Saudi Arabia) in 2034."

The news about the 2030 World Cup had already been known for some time. There were two bids—the Euro-African and the South American. The FIFA board decided to give the World Cup to both. Something like this has not happened in the history of football, and many suspected that the award paves the way for the World Cup 2034 to go to one confederation: Asia. This is due to FIFA's rotation rule that the World Cup must rotate between the world's continents. The deadline to submit a bid was October 31, and it was expected that Australia (a member of the Asian Football Confederation) might apply. However, after experiencing significant pressure from other nations, Australia decided not to apply. Thus, only one country remained: Saudi Arabia.

We remember the situation in January, when Cristiano Ronaldo was the only top player in the country. Now we are in November 2023. He has been followed by Riyad Mahrez, Karim Benzema, Sadio Mané, Roberto Firmino, Jordan Henderson, Neymar, Aymeric Laporte and a host of other players—all of whom potentially with many years left in world-class football. A disclosed point in these contracts is that the players are not allowed to criticise the country. Another part of the contract of many of these players is that they have to promote Saudi Arabia in different contexts, and this was done by former Liverpool player Henderson, who previously has held the rainbow flag high in many situations. But in Saudi Arabia, homosexuality is a criminal act and can result in the death penalty, as happened when 37 men were mass executed in 2019. Five of them were accused of "same-sex acts", with one of them tortured into confessing. Henderson promoted the country's World Cup bid.

"What do you think about the way Saudi Arabia won the World Cup in 1934?"

"We are very critical towards FIFA's process, not only for the 2034 World Cup, but also 2030. We try to understand what really happened. It will probably be a difficult job to get someone to go against what happened and try to change something. I have been in this world for a while now, and I know that criticising such a consensus-based decision is challenging," says Klaveness, before she tries to analyse the course of events and what FIFA and Infantino actually did.

"It is not necessarily outside the rules. But they have stretched the rules quite a bit. Although the decision formally sits in the FIFA Congress, it has already been decided. Then the power does not really lie with the congress, even though this should be FIFA's most democratic body. The power is located somewhere else, and we do not have access to this place. Everyone has seen the movements that Saudi Arabia has lobbied. There is nothing surprising about that. But at the same time, it is surprising, because it shows that there has been a lot of rigging in the shades," she says.

When Infantino was elected in 2016, FIFA launched several reforms. The aim was to "rebuild trust" after the arrests during the congress in 2015 when president Sepp Blatter had to leave due to alleged corruption. The organisation was to become more open and transparent, and the World Cup was to be awarded by the FIFA Congress and not by the FIFA board.

"They clearly promised reforms when Gianni was elected. A written reform, which changed the statutes and allocation processes radically, to provide more insight and distribution of power."

"Which is something real democracies need."

"Yes, in a complex landscape, to ensure that you are responsible for someone. Now, in practice, it is the opposite. It doesn't help to have a thoroughly designed process if everything in practice happens in the back room. For all we know, Gianni has worked actively to get many bids, but it could also be the opposite, that FIFA has worked actively to remove all other bids. Just to calm things down. We cannot know. It is serious, in itself this is a violation of the intention behind the reform."

"I'm saying things that are obvious to public opinion, but internally everyone's position is that you cannot do anything about it anyway. If you do, you only get FIFA against you. But I don't know what else we can do. We cannot mobilise from within when things like this happen again and again. If we don't speak out ourselves, and be transparent, we won't get change anyway. We football leaders cannot work to get an important reform passed about transparency, accountability and human rights, and then afterwards all federations sit still when the reform isn't complied with. Then we become a political cartel," she says.

In addition to having the death penalty for homosexuality, Saudi Arabia also has a lack of free speech and working conditions that are similar to those in Qatar. But it is not the case that countries that violate human rights cannot host the World Cup—then other host countries would not be relevant either. However, according to its own statutes, FIFA is obliged *not* to contribute to the violation of human rights in connection with its own events. This means that everyone who in one way or another works with World Cup preparations must have their rights secured. This was not the case in Qatar according to Amnesty and Human Rights Watch, as well as other organisations.

"It's important to be equally engaged in the awarding to Spain/Morocco/Portugal as to Saudi Arabia. What must now be done is that we must get an independent assessment of the human rights situation in these countries. A report showing whether there is a risk of human rights violations in connection with the World Cup. Just creating the report will be challenging for Saudi Arabia. As it was for Qatar. Just dealing with trade unions, and more or less independent organisations, was challenging in Qatar. It requires a commitment from FIFA just to produce such a report," she says.

The question is whether Klaveness can get help from other nations when this criticism of the process is to be developed through actions.

"Perhaps there is not much to be gained in the cooperation between the Nordic countries? At least not if it's still the way it was in May, with the situation you described from the Faroe Islands?"

"It was awful. There has always been political tension, and I have not known the background to it. And I think the reactions I got to what I have done have been downright unreasonable. But now I feel that since I am no longer running for election, we have put it behind us. It is much better now, and the main reason is that they have got a new secretary general. He comes from the government; seems to be a vigilant person," says Klaveness.

In other words, it seems as if Norway and Denmark are playing on the same team again in this matter.

"Denmark and Norway cannot do anything alone. Obviously, other confederations are also good at working internally, such as England and the Netherlands. But when a process has been so closed, the work you do internally is not enough. Denmark also wants to discuss the awarding of the 2034 World Cup. Then we are two countries. That's one more than last year, when we were alone. Denmark will join us in Qatar too," she says.

Qatar?

Yes, 18 months after her famous speech and a year after the World Cup, Lise Klaveness will return to Doha.

A Year Uphill

Before we move on to Qatar, let's take a look at how 2023 has unfolded.

Lise Klaveness was not elected to the UEFA board. The Nordic countries did not get hosting rights for the European Championship in 2025. Even though Norway's proposal in Kigali was accepted, FIFA will not provide any information about the sub-committee for human rights and the committee has apparently done nothing. Infantino may have broken the rules when he gave the 2034 World Cup to Saudi Arabia. The cooperation between the Nordic countries has not gone smoothly, and out on the pitch the year has been bleak. We will not make it to the men's Euros, and the women's World Cup was a failure. Nor did the women manage to qualify for the Olympics, and they might be relegated to the second division in the Nations League.

"How would you sum up the year, yourself?"

"Now the year is not over. At times, I think the way you do, it's been some tough fights," she says in mid-November, referring to the points mentioned above.

"The next [few] days we are facing international matches which may not be important for qualification," she says.

The men's team face the Faroe Islands in a private match, and then Scotland in the final qualifying match. The women face Portugal and Austria in the Nations League.

"But we are football people. For us, it is important to get a good feeling in those matches. At the same time, it is also important to find out how we as a federation can show support to those who provide help for those who suffer in the Middle East, with small things and big things. But I understand your question. I am just as passionate about the match against the Faroe Islands as I am about a World Cup match. That's how I was as a player, too. In the memories, a World Cup match is bigger, but the feeling around the game is the same. For the women, it has been tough for several years. Because the situation out there is escalating. Portugal is good, very good. They weren't before. It has also been tough because of the situation with Hege," she says.

She is referring to Hege Riise, the national team coach who had to leave after the Oceania World Cup.

"Nevertheless, this autumn we've played well until now, even though the results don't reflect that. The development has been good, but if it doesn't end up with good results, the girls will go to the Christmas break without having nailed the last few games."

"What about football politics in 2023?"

"It's been tough. We knew I wasn't going to be elected, but we still wanted to follow the debate about women's representation and break that barrier. We have done that. Many of us worked hard towards something that, seen from the outside, ended in nothing. But we've had conversations with 55 countries who thought it was strange that we did not simply run for the designated women's place on the board. We have learned a lot, and perhaps we have given others some perspectives as well. We've suffered some losses, taken a few hits. It was a big disappointment that we didn't get the Euro 2025, as was the change of coach for the women's team, and the men not qualifying for the Euros. These are big, heavy defeats. The economy too, everything becomes more expensive for the grassroots football. But that's the kind of thing that makes us addicted too. Like a child, I'm looking forward to every football match, every club meeting or tournament. We have a core activity that is fun. This is important to remember."

"Norway must find a position where we focus on our opportunities.

We can't do anything about the fact that we're small, that it's cold, that we don't have the same money as Manchester City. But we have other strengths. Compared to others, we work closely together, we trust each other, we have gender equality and so on. We are a small fish in a big ocean. The question is: how are we going to swim?"

Qatar 2023

The first thing she does after this conversation is to go to Qatar. We're at the end of November. Klaveness, advisor Borgen and the rest of the team have tried to organise the trip throughout the autumn, but the work hasn't been easy. One aim for the trip is to follow up the initiative at the FIFA Congress in Kigali. What does the legacy after the World Cup 2022 look like after one year? Are the labour rights reforms being implemented, as FIFA and Qatar claim? Are there fewer violations of human rights? Are the safety and rights of workers at the World Cup arenas safeguarded?

The NFF contacted a number of other federations in order to create a larger travelling party. The interest was lukewarm. At the same time, they tried to find out more about the sub-committee for human rights that was announced in Kigali by FIFA and Infantino with a bang. However, there is zero public information about it, and the NFF had to compile its own internal overview of the members of the committee. This list includes Swiss football president Dominique Blanc; Mukul Mudgal, an Indian lawyer; Christopher Mihm, an American bureaucrat and expert on governance, overlap, duplication, and fragmentation; Edibayou Dassoundo from Benin, a lawyer and leader of the women's referees' association in the West African country; Paul Cochrane from New Zealand, who, in addition to having served in the country's football association, has also been head of its postal service. The last on the NFF's list is Juan Manuel Iglesias from Argentina, who, like Mudgal and Llamas, is already in the FIFA system—all three of them also have seats in FIFA's governance, audit and compliance committee.

I've contacted FIFA several times to get information about the sub-committee for human rights and its work, but the response from media spokesperson Adam Steiss has been: "Thanks for your email, I confirm receipt and will get back to you with any information to share." My colleagues from *Josimar* have all done the same, with the same answer.

There are many indications that the committee has not worked very intensively, and the work it has possibly done cannot possibly be said to have been high profile.

Nevertheless, when Klaveness, Løken and Borgen arrive in Doha on November 27, together with Norwegian trade union leader Steinar Krogstad, one other nation joins the trip: Denmark, represented by their new secretary general Erik Brøgger Rasmussen.

"They were actually in the World Cup, they experienced it. That's good, because we have to keep it related to football. We can't get anything done in Qatar, change anything, but we can keep our word. We said we were going back. Now we keep highlighting what is important. The World Cup, the kafala [construction workers'] system, workers' rights and so on. It's easier to get the right impression of this on the ground than through a PC screen."

But like the football associations the NFF has contacted, the response from the Qatari authorities and institutions has been slow. Only one official meeting is secured: with the ILO (International Labor Organisation), a UN organisation that works to secure workers' rights worldwide. In Qatar, this means (among other things) to monitor whether the allegedly implemented reforms regarding working conditions are *really* implemented.

Before and during the World Cup, many questioned the neutrality of the reports coming from ILO. The reason was the financial partnership between Qatar and ILO in the years leading up to the championship. During this period, Qatar paid for all of the ILO's missions in the country.

In addition, Klaveness wants a meeting with the Qatar Football Association and with former World Cup boss Hassan Al-Thawadi—and not least, to also meet some migrants who worked for the World Cup organisers.

But all this is "to be confirmed", and the first thing that happens is that the almost-agreed-upon meeting at 09:00 in the morning is cancelled by the Qatari FA. It's just as well, the NFF instead uses the extra time to get to know Denmark's new secretary general better. They go to the Lusail Stadium where the 2022 World Cup final was played, and the lopsided relationship between Norway and Denmark seems to be back on track.

✳ ✳ ✳

At the same time, in the part of town called the Industrial Area that's deep in Doha's concrete jungle, two young Gambians (Amadou and Bubacarr) sign a document at the exit of the boarding school where they live. The signatures confirm that they will meet 'a friend' and that they will be back by 6 p.m. Neither Amadou or Bubacarr have passports, papers, money or jobs, and essentially, they have to spend all their time at the shelter they've been staying in for almost a year.

Amadou turned 17 two days prior. Bubacarr is 19. Both lived normal lives as children back home in The Gambia. But in 2016, the country got a new president and government. Until then, school had been free, but the new regime changed this policy. Amadou and Bubacarr are related, and their families could not afford to pay school fees. They started working in the forestry industry at Bansang village like their fathers. They sold timber to a Chinese company, but disagreements soon arose between the Chinese and the authorities. Sustainable forestry was one issue they couldn't agree upon. In the end, the Chinese company left The Gambia, and both Amadou and Bubacarr's families were without work. Shortly after, Amadou's father died, and in their mid-teens they both were suddenly the main breadwinners of their families.

At the same time, advertisements started to appear on social media, other parts of the internet and traditional media: there was an abundance of jobs available in Qatar. The main reason was the upcoming World Cup. The organisers needed people for stadium construction, infrastructure, security and a general upgrade of the entire city of Doha. If you signed an agency contract for around 2,500 euros, your agent would obtain your visa and plane ticket, and put you in touch with a company in Qatar that would provide you with food, accommodation and a salary.

The families of Amadou and Bubacarr owned some land, but the soil was dry and not suitable for cultivation. At times, the Saharan winds from the North East turned the area into a dust bowl. They therefore decided to sell the land, move the families to the town of Brikama and use the rest of the profits to pay the agent's fee. In 2022, Amadou and Bubacarr each boarded a plane to Doha with new passports. They had not been abroad before. The dates of birth on their passports had been changed by the networks of the agents, so that, for example, 15-year-old Amadou appeared as a 22-year-old, and thus was old enough to work legally. Amadou came in March, Bubacarr in July. The contracts said they were to work as delivery boys.

When they landed in Qatar, they were directed to accommodation where they shared a room with several others. Their supposed delivery boy jobs didn't exist, and they didn't get any other work either. After conversations with other migrant workers, they quickly realised that the contracts they had signed in The Gambia meant nothing. Everywhere they went in Qatar, they met workers with similar experiences. Bubacarr never got hold of his agent, and Amadou eventually started working as a construction worker at Stadium 974. The World Cup arena was assembled from containers, only to be dismantled after the championship and forwarded to another country and tournament—according to the original plan, it was sent to Africa somewhere.

"Up to nine hours a day, seven days a week," says Amadou about his days building Stadium 974.

I meet the boys in Doha's Industrial Area. The agreement is that Klaveness will come here and meet them as soon as the meeting with the ILO in the city centre is finished.

Before the World Cup, they signed six-month employment contracts with Stark Security, a company that provided a number of services to World Cup organisers. They got jobs as security guards, and the QNCC (Qatar National Convention Centre) was their headquarters. From there, they were sent to different locations, wherever they were needed.

"When we signed the papers that gave us the ID cards showing we were World Cup workers, FIFA said: 'If you experience any kind of problems, come back to us, we will help you,'" says Bubacarr.

Both of them ended up at Stadium 974 several times during the World Cup.

"We had to keep our eyes on the audience the whole time. If we turned around to see the match, we would be deported," he says. A threat was always hanging over migrant workers in Qatar, who often, like Amadou and Bubacarr, had spent the entire savings of their families just to pay their agents to get a job. Other workers didn't have that kind of money, and ended up borrowing money from their agents, which resulted in endless debts that were paid through extra shifts in the Qatar heat.

After a day at work just after the World Cup final where their job had been to collect equipment used during the championship, Amadou and Bubacarr were contacted by Stark Security.

"They said: 'Your services are no longer needed, you can collect your things and have to leave your place of residence,'" says Amadou.

Stark Security also demanded that they sign a document stating that they had been paid all wages and had settled all agreements with the company. However, a group of 200 workers who received these messages banded together and protested. They claimed the company owed them 8,000 Qatari rials, which is around 2,000 euros. The organisers of this collective action were subsequently arrested and/or deported.

"The police said they had organised demonstrations, and that is not allowed in Qatar, but there were no demonstrations," says Bubacarr.

The rest of the 200 had to leave their respective places of residence. For Amadou and Bubacarr, that meant being homeless. For two or three weeks they moved around, sleeping in the streets of the Industrial Area before they were given a place in a state-run shelter.

"We had to give up our passports and all our personal documents to live there, and we had to sign some papers. I don't know what was written on them, it was in Arabic," says Bubacarr.

Then, they decided to sue Stark Securities.

"But we were told that Stark Securities no longer existed," says Amadou.

The message came from Fatma Al Kuwari, who ran the boarding school where they lived. Stark Securities is a subsidiary of Estithmar Holding Group, and Al Kuwari has three relatives who sit on Estithmar's board. Stark was one of FIFA's partners during the World Cup.[2]

"That's why we took legal action against our agents and the companies they represent instead," Amadou continues as we get a message from the NFF saying that they won't be able to get to the Industrial Area after all, due to a change of plans. A state secretary from the Qatari

---

[2] This story was also reported in Josimar, the football magazine where the author of this book works. The article was written by Samindra Kunti. Estithmar Holding was offered a chance to comment upon the charges. They never answered the questions they were sent.

Ministry of Labour did not want to be present at the planned meeting between the ILO and the NFF. Instead, she asked for a separate meeting with Klaveness, which she got.

Magnus Borgen tries to move their program around to ensure the meeting with Amadou and Bubacarr will happen. He suggests we meet later in the day, either at Stadium 974 or near the hotel where the NFF attendees are staying. The boys, the photographer and I get into an Uber, drive towards the city, and sit down on some benches a couple of hundred metres away from the hotel to wait.

The meeting between the NFF and the state secretary takes time, but Amadou and Bubacarr are used to waiting. It's almost a year since they had any work, and seven or eight months since they went to trial. They aren't allowed to work; they largely spend their days staring at the ceiling. On weekends, they are forced to stay inside the state-run shelter all the time. On weekdays, they can be granted short trips out but only if they provide a very good reason and present it to "Madame". That's what they call the head of the shelter, Fatma Al Kuwari.

"But we must have a driver with us who looks after everything we do. Today we were lucky, the driver was going to accompany some female workers, domestic workers. They had to go somewhere, so we were allowed to go alone. We said we were going to meet a friend from The Gambia who was going back to our homeland," says Amadou.

Finally, Klaveness and Borgen come out of the hotel, accompanied by Steinar Krogstad from the trade union. Klaveness is excited about the meeting she's just had with the state secretary.

"She comes from the Supreme Committee [for Delivery & Legacy]. It turns out that many of the people who work there have been transferred to the Ministry of Labour. Obviously, she has her objectives. She wants to show that the changes they have talked about have actually happened. But she is informal, you can talk to her," says Klaveness.

Then she approaches the boys who tell their story, right up to their trial.

"But I have just been in a meeting with a state secretary," says Klaveness. "She told me about the new arrangements. They have made it possible for everyone to file their cases digitally. Have you done it? Did you file the case digitally?" Klaveness asks.

"No," replies Amadou. "But we have been to court many times."

At regular intervals, the boys are told to appear at a court office in central Doha. There they are asked to sign an Arabic document that they do not understand. Then they are told that their case is still in the system. They must go home and wait further.

"We've probably been there seven or eight times now," says Amadou.

The conversation between Klaveness and the boys continues. She digs into the details and tries to figure out exactly what has happened. The boys are not allowed to work. They have no money and no personal documents. They are awaiting trial. They must stay indoors. They want to get paid the money Stark and the agents owe them. They cannot afford tickets home. And as long as their case is in the juridical system, they're not allowed to leave the country at all, even if Qatar paid for their tickets. And what about FIFA, who promised to help?

"We contacted them, and they said they would get back to us. Since then, we haven't heard anything," says Bubacarr.[3]

After about half-an-hour's friendly conversation, both parties must move on. Klaveness has her appointments, and we're getting close to the time when the boys must return to Madame. The NFF president says that it is outside her mandate to pursue individual cases of World Cup workers. She nevertheless promises to proceed with Amadou and

---

[3] As Estithmar, FIFA was also asked why they didn't help the boys as they had promised. FIFA answered through this statement: "FIFA, in collaboration with its Qatari counterparts, implemented a far-reaching due diligence process with the aim to ensure that companies involved in FIFA World Cup-related construction and services abide by the Supreme Committee's Workers' Welfare Standards. We consider any non-compliance with these standards unacceptable and are actively following up when we learn about alleged breaches.

It is the primary responsibility of the respective companies as well as the Qatari authorities to rectify possible adverse impacts on workers. As FIFA, we work to use our leverage with the relevant entities to promote the provision of remedy when we become aware of such allegations, in line with our responsibilities under international standards. This also includes the steps taken to help address the situation of Stark Security which involved SC [Supreme Committee], the ILO and the Qatari Ministry of Labour. We kindly refer you to the SC and the ILO for further information on the specific case."

Bubacarr's case, with help from Steinar Krogstad and the trade union network. The first step is to find out exactly where the case stands in the system. Now everyone must leave, and this is done with a kind of agreement to meet for a 'kickabout' in The Gambia sometime in the future. Klaveness says she is "pretty good", the boys say they're "not too bad either", they were on the winning team in a workers' tournament held during the World Cup. Klaveness then jokes that this little five-a-side kickabout in The Gambia might not be a good idea after all, and they say their goodbyes with smiles on their faces.

On the way back to the Industrial Area, we stop at what was once Stadium 974. The plans to send the entire stadium to Africa have been put on hold. Now there is talk of sending it to Uruguay instead for the big jubilee matches in 2030 when the 100th anniversary of the World Cup tournament will be celebrated. Amadou and Bubacarr walk towards the stadium which they helped build as construction workers and later helped protect as security guards. Now the arena is half dismantled. The lower rows of containers are still present, while the upper ones have been replaced by gaping holes. Maybe the containers are in Africa, maybe they are somewhere else. Then Bubacarr's phone rings. It's Madame, who says that there's only an hour until their curfew starts. If they're not on their way home already, they better get on the move now.

The meeting between Klaveness and Hassan Al-Thawadi, the head of the Supreme Committee, did not materialise.

"But he called. He said he hadn't even heard that there was going to be a meeting," says Klaveness.

It's late in the evening, and she's slightly puzzled by the ex-World Cup boss's explanation.

"In any case, he is a man who answers you if you ask him questions," she says, although the answers she received about Qatar's implementation of reforms to human rights and working conditions don't seem to have been surprising.

The NFF president is going home to Norway that night, and she's relatively satisfied with the visit.

"We get knowledge from being here. We have spoken to workers and others from the Qatari authorities. On paper, there is no decline after the World Cup. But the implementation of the reforms lags, sometimes very much. We, as leaders of the NFF, are required by our international strategy to be knowledge-based. Even though it was only one day, I do feel that we have learned a lot," she says.

"Another thing is the fact that FIFA has promised to follow up on the reforms, and its own obligations with regard to the workers' human rights."

"How does it feel to be the one person from FIFA who goes down there to do this part of the job?"

"No, that's not how it should be. FIFA and the sub-committee for human rights must deliver a report by the end of December. The work on it was meant to be transparent, but instead there is no transparency around it at all. So, we must pay attention to that," she says.

Among the cases the NFF discussed in Qatar was Abdullah Ibhais, the former head of communications for the World Cup committee, who in 2021 was imprisoned after notifying that the committee was spreading false news about worker demonstrations in the country.

"What we are asking now is whether he gets health care. You are entitled to that in Qatari prisons. They say he gets that kind of health care. But the reports we get say the opposite," she says.

"What about his actual case?"

"He is convicted. We cannot change the judiciary here."

"No. But you can discuss the background for his imprisonment?"

"True. And we do that. But now, for our part, it was mostly about whether he gets health care."

This trip to Doha also represents a flashback to when Klaveness gave her famous speech. At that time, she also stayed at this hotel.

"I didn't know anyone. Not Jesper Møller, not Karl Erik Nilsson. I remember we were right here," she says, pointing around the dark, elegant garden of the hotel.

"Then, I remember, I got a feeling of being visible in a completely new environment, in a very negative way."

"I noticed that people started talking to each other. A rumour was circulating that someone from Northern Europe was going to take the podium and say something. Finally, Alexandre Čeferin came over to me, and asked what was going on. I was completely new, and I got the feeling of being somewhere I wasn't welcome," she says.

"Like a fish out of water?"

"Like a fish out of water. And all those feelings come back, when I'm here, in the same place, now."

More really good football books from Fair Play Publishing

George Best Down Under

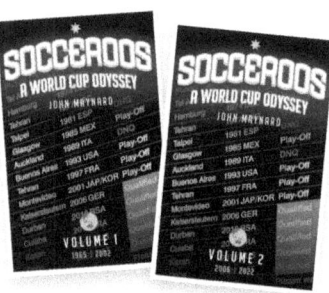
Socceroos – A World Cup Odyssey, 1965 to 2022 Volumes 1 and 2

"Get Your Tits Out for the Lads"

The First Matildas The 1975 Asian Ladies Championship

Hear Us Roar – An anthology of emerging women football writers

Whatever It Takes - the Inside Story of the FIFA Way

Available from fairplaypublishing.com.au/shop and all good bookstores

fairplaypublishing.com.au

www.ingramcontent.com/pod-product-compliance
Lightning Source LLC
Chambersburg PA
CBHW041318110526
44591CB00021B/2833